How to Be Happy in Life Alone

VIVIAN GREY

© Copyright 2020 Vivian Grey

All Rights Reserved

This document is geared towards providing exact and reliable information, with regards to the topic and issue covered. The publication is sold with the idea that the publisher is not required to render accounting, officially permitted, or otherwise, qualified services. If advice is necessary, legal or professional, the services of a practiced individual in the profession should be considered.

From a Declaration of Principles which was accepted and approved equally by a Committee of the American Bar Association and a Committee of Publishers and Associations.

In no way is it legal to reproduce, duplicate, or transmit any part of this document, in either electronic means or printed format. Recording of this publication is strictly prohibited and any storage of this document is not allowed unless with written permission from the publisher. All rights reserved.

The information provided herein is stated to be truthful and consistent, in that any liability, in terms of inattention or otherwise, by any usage or abuse of any policies, processes, or directions contained within is the solitary and utter responsibility of the recipient reader. Under no circumstances will any legal responsibility or blame be held against the publisher for any reparation, damages, or monetary loss due to the information herein, either directly or indirectly.

Respective authors own all copyrights not held by the publisher.

The information herein is offered for informational purposes solely, and is universal as so. The presentation of the information is without contract or any type of guarantee assurance.

The trademarks that are used are without any consent, and the publication of the trademark is without permission or backing by the trademark owner. All trademarks and brands within this book are for clarifying purposes only and are the owned by the owners themselves, not affiliated with this document.

Table of Contents

INTRODUCTION --- 6

CHAPTER 1: PRACTICE LOVE FOR YOURSELF --------------------- 10

SELF ESTEEM -- 11
HOW TO INCREASE SELF-ESTEEM (STEP BY STEP) ------------------------ 21
FORGIVE YOURSELF --- 23
5 AFFIRMATIONS THAT HELP YOU FORGIVE YOURSELF ------------------ 25
PROTECT AND TAKE CARE OF YOURSELF ------------------------- 38

CHAPTER 2: USEFUL TIPS --- 41

TRAIN AND MEDITATE -- 41
READ, STUDY AND INFORM YOURSELF ------------------------------------ 42
SURROUND YOURSELF WITH POSITIVITY ---------------------------------- 43
CREATE A HEALTHY AND BALANCED ROUTINE --------------------------- 44
CONCLUSION: LOVE YOURSELF AND TAKE CARE OF YOURSELF ---------- 46
12 PHRASES YOU MUST BE ABLE TO SAY TO YOURSELF EVERY DAY ------ 47

CHAPTER 3: VIEW LIFE ON A POSITIVE SIDE AS A SINGLE ----- 55

10 MORE REASONS WHY LIVING ALONE IS JUST GREAT: ------------------ 56
15 REASONS WHY YOU SHOULD LIVE ALONE AT LEAST ONCE IN YOUR LIFE
-- 58
7 TIPS TO BETTER MANAGE TOO MUCH FREE TIME WHEN LIVING QUARANTINE ALONE --- 65

LIVING ALONE: 4 MAIN RESPONSIBILITIES TO FACE. -----------------68

CHAPTER 4: SPEND MORE TIME WITH YOUR FAMILY AND FRIENDS --70

HOW TO MAKE YOUR FAMILY UNDERSTAND THAT YOU ARE SINGLE BUT NOT ALONE AND DESPERATE--74
I'M THE ONLY SINGLE IN A GROUP OF PAIRED FRIENDS -------------------79

CHAPTER 5: COMFORT ZONE - THE BEGINNING OF YOUR LIFE --83

CHAPTER 6: ENJOY YOUR FREEDOM -------------------------------88

BELOW I OFFER YOU 25 (TWENTY-FIVE!) PRACTICAL TIPS TO BE HAPPY ALONE --90

CHAPTER 7: STARTING A NEW HOBBY BY BEING SINGLE ------95

7 CREATIVE HOBBIES TO START AT HOME -----------------------101

CHAPTER 8: TYPES OF SINGLE MEN AND WHY THEY LIKE TO LIVE ALONE --111

CHAPTER 9: APPRECIATE LIFE------------------------------------114

PART 1: CHANGING PERSPECTIVE ----------------------------------114
PART 2: CHANGE YOUR ACTIONS -----------------------------------119
PART 3: NEW BEGINNING--123

CHAPTER 10: RECOGNIZE THE IMPORTANCE OF PERFECT TIMING---127

Personal flowering and the secret of perfume ------------------138

CHAPTER 11: HOW NOT TO SUFFER FROM LONELINESS?---142

Emotional Independence ---142

CHAPTER 12: RECOGNIZE THE IMPORTANCE OF THE PERFECT MOMENT WHEN YOU ARE SINGLE --------------------------------152

CHAPTER 13: HOW TO GROW PROFESSIONALLY TO ADVANCE YOUR CAREER (AND YOUR BUSINESS) ---------------------------161

Tips for growing professionally-------------------------------------164

CHAPTER 14: POSITIVE MENTAL ATTITUDE ----------------------170

Mental Exercises to Train You to Think Positive ----------------171

CHAPTER 15: THE WAY OF SUCCESS -------------------------------176

CONCLUSION --182

Being alone and the effects on the brain --------------------------187

INTRODUCTION

CAN YOU BE HAPPY ALONE?
SURE! I WILL EXPLAIN HOW

Being happy alone is possible!

When we think of the concept of happiness in relation to that of loneliness, the first thought that comes to mind is that of being single or being in a relationship. However, we do not know that it is not the same thing. It is clear to everyone that living alone is not necessarily the same as living in isolation or solitude.

Usually, we deliberately surround ourselves with people, even though we do not have a partner—friends, family members, work colleagues, or superficial acquaintances, with whom we interact, mostly due to unavoidable social routines.

Today, unless you lock yourself indoors from morning to night, being completely alone is not exactly obtainable in such a crowded world. From the moment you are born, you are surrounded by people—family, family friends and medical practitioners.

Since childhood, we have learned that man is a social animal and needs to surround himself with a group of equals. We understood this before learning the art of being alone. Perhaps, this may be the reason why the thought of being by ourselves frightens us sometimes, giving us that sense of dependence on others.

When we begin to evolve as individuals, the need for us to be alone arises; we finally realize the most important person in the world: Our very own selves. . Most people, however, are not yet ready to accept this condition, to cultivate themselves and know themselves more deeply.

This is also why, oftentimes, we make the mistake of throwing ourselves into the arms of the first person we come across, even though not yet ready for such commitment, believing that the relationship can compensate for the emptiness we feel inside. Other obvious reasons could be due to the spirit of emulation as well as social impositions.

The real point is that today, in 2020, there are still women who are convinced that a woman without a man is of very little value, or worse—useless. It's true, and I confirm it: Happiness when shared with someone (for example, a couple) is multiplied. Although, this can only be when both partners are already complete, satisfied, and autonomous.

How to be happy alone

To feel good about ourselves, we must understand that the most important person on earth is us.

This is a form of healthy selfishness with which we understand an essential principle: If we are not well, no one else will be well. It is only when we fall in love with us that everything begins to shine with a stronger and more decisive light. Being alone in a conscious way unleashes many unexplored potentials, including the most powerful force ever known by mankind: Autonomy.

Being autonomous means being free, and being free means no longer depending on anyone. When addiction no longer exists, we can make conscious choices, as there are no longer any constraints. It is then that past needs will turn into desires, and we can finally start conquering the world around us, bubbling with newfound self-esteem and awareness of our potential.

Some practical tips for feeling good alone

Those who are happy alone know that it does not take much to remain in this state of mind. The journey is more important than the destination, which should be a little scary; but if we consider that time is on our side—with patience and constancy—we can make this treasure our own.

The first step (and perhaps also the final goal) should be to fall in love with us again.

We begin to take care of our physical appearance.

The physical aspect is important and, despite what you think, it is not only the mirror of what you have inside but also your self-reflection. By changing the outside, the inside changes.

Let's start taking care of the external environment. To feel good alone, we need a suitable environment to do it.

Do you live in a chaotic environment and cannot be at peace with yourself? Look around. Your home and/ or work environment likely reflects this.

Change what surrounds you, and you will begin to change too. We start taking care of relationships. Being happy alone, as mentioned, does not mean becoming a hermit. Social relationships are necessary—one of the most important aspects to take into account during this transformation, in order to generate new awareness.

Relationships constitute an effective test bed to verify the starting point and the progress of one's path. Affective addictions, need for social feedback, excessive consideration of opinions generated from outside, etc. can be a clear symptom that something in your life is not going right.

Do you have to change friendships, partners, boyfriends or whatever?

Absolutely not!

Oftentimes, we will realize during our journey, that the actors will not necessarily change, but the part we will assign them in our life will certainly change, as we have become the only directors.

We begin to observe ourselves.

Consider this piece of advice that will make a difference in your life: Start looking at what you do with different eyes. Create the *Witness*, an element that looks at how you behave from the outside, "depersonalizing" your every single action and behavior. We are so entangled in the reality that surrounds us, that with difficulty, we are truly aware of what we do. Furthermore, even though we are one person, in you and me, there are very different and changing realities.

The Witness will help you better understand who you are in every area of your life.

Being happy alone, therefore, can and must.

CHAPTER 1: Practice Love for Yourself

Embrace yourself

Embrace yourself and you will be able to contain the rest of the world

Hug yourself until you feel the warmth of being accepted. Enjoy that unexpected squeeze that comes when you feel the need and know how to welcome it because you finally give yourself the necessary love. Your heart is what you feel and it has always spoken to you; too many times, it has been forced to scream, but now it can beat without difficulty.

Your hands must seek and find you; do not leave them unsatisfied, they know how to be full of you and caress you like no one can even imagine doing. Ally with your desires and recognize them. This is the best place to ferment. Forgive yourself for having invested your senses elsewhere, leaving you mute and blind, at the mercy of an indifference you never deserved. Too many times, you have invoked the name of people too far away, tearing up your own that remained to contain memory and projects.

Love yourself. If you learn to do it without compromise, the distance between you and the world will shorten, without uncomfortable invasions. You are the one who designs your living spaces, you define the necessary boundaries. Open your world to those who want to enter it barefoot. Offer yourself a strong shoulder, on which to rest your tearful cheek; if you know how to dry it, you will teach the other how to caress your soul and leave it with a smile.

Listen to yourself because in this way, you will know the right words to grant your voice. Those who listen to you will also recognize the weight of your "unspoken" and will be able to translate them into concern. If your embrace will be able to fill you, it will only leave the necessary space for someone else to enter, gracefully and with respect.

Love yourself and you will be loved, because you will have learned to choose who can reach your heart, deserving its every beat.

I encourage you to believe in yourself

Self-esteem

Self-esteem is believing in yourself and your potential. It is a process that leads each of us to evaluate and appreciate our own qualities. Self-esteem is built step by step every day, coming into contact with our deepest values.

Expressing judgments about yourself is never an easy task as it implies a certain amount of honesty. Those who have self-esteem have in fact, the ability to realistically recognize their strengths and weaknesses and put themselves out there to improve.

Here is an inspirational guide on self-esteem that can make you think about the topic:

1. Every winner I've ever met says, "My life changed when I started believing in myself."
2. The length of the limousine is inversely proportional to the self-esteem of the person driving it.
3. Every morning I wake up and looking in the mirror, I always feel the same, immense pleasure—that of being Salvador Dalí.
4. Whoever loses money, loses a lot; whoever loses a friend loses much more; whoever loses self-confidence, loses everything.
5. Wanting to be someone else is a waste of who you are.
6. Self-esteem is the fuel to make our dreams come true.
7. When no one believes in you, you believe in yourself.
8. Forget everything pedants have taught you. Convince yourself that nothing is impossible for you. Think yourself able to understand everything: The arts, the sciences, and the nature of every living being.
9. Having high self-esteem is a feeling appropriate to life.
10. Sit in the sun. Abdicate and be king of yourself.
11. Don't worry if others don't like you. Worry if you don't appreciate yourself.
12. Too much self-esteem leads to arrogance, low self-esteem leads to self-contempt. The wise know how to keep themselves in the middle ground between these two poles.

13. That you believe in yourself when a hundred people don't believe, is much more important than the fact that a hundred people believe in you than you do.
14. I believe in myself. I believe I can accomplish anything.
15. The power of dreams and the influence of the human spirit should never be underestimated. We are all equal in this light. Inside each of us, there is the seed of a potential that can make us great.
16. No one can force you to feel inferior without your consent.
17. Many of us go through life like failures, because we are waiting for the 'right time' to start doing something useful. Do not wait. The moment can never be the 'right' one. Start where you are, and work with whatever tools you may have available, and you will find better tools as you go along.
18. It is lack of faith that makes people fearful of taking on a challenge, and I have always had faith: In fact, I believe in myself.
19. I don't think I'm beautiful. But, what value does my humble opinion have against what the mirror declares instead?
20. If you can't be a highway, be a path. If you can't be the sun, be a star. Always be the best of who you are.
21. Face obstacles and do something to overcome them. You'll find they don't even have half the strength you thought they had.
22. Self-esteem is the deepest content of human life.
23. The main task in everyone's life is to give birth to himself.
24. If I have lost faith in myself, I have the universe against me.
25. The worst loneliness is not feeling good about yourself.

26. For people who do not esteem themselves, success is zero, failure is double.
27. Remove the "not" from the "I cannot."
28. For once, you believed in yourself. You thought you were beautiful and so did the rest of the world.
29. If you don't believe in yourself, who will believe?
30. You will always meet people who will try to belittle your successes. Try not to be the first to do it.
31. Before diagnosing yourself with depression or low self-esteem, make sure you're not just surrounded by assholes.
32. Why should we care what others think of us, why should we trust their opinions more than ours?
33. When you are different, sometimes you don't see those millions of people who accept you for who you are. All you notice is that one person who doesn't.
34. As long as you look to others to prove who you are and seek their approval, you are setting up your life in a disastrous way. You have to be complete on your own. Nobody can give you this. You have to know who you are. What others say is irrelevant.
35. Be beautiful, and if possible, wise. However, respect yourself; this is essential.
36. The core of your personality is self-esteem, "how much you like yourself." The more you like and respect yourself, the better you will do in whatever you want to undertake.
37. Whoever values himself is safe from others; he wears a breastplate that no one can penetrate.
38. You can have what you want if you are willing to get rid of the belief that you cannot.
39. Self-esteem is the cornerstone of all virtues.
40. Dare to become what you are. Don't disarm easily. There are wonderful opportunities in every being.

Convince yourself of your strength and your youth. It keeps repeating incessantly: "It's not up to me."

41. Accept yourself as you are in this moment; an imperfect, changeable, growing and respectable person.
42. Some people have so much respect for their superiors that they have no longer kept any for themselves.
43. Esteem yourself. The only ones who appreciate a doormat are those with dirty shoes.
44. Don't be bullied silently. Don't let them make a victim of you. Don't accept anyone's definition of your life, define yourself.
45. Until you appreciate yourself, you don't value your time. Until you value your time, you won't do anything with it.
46. When you are happy to be yourself and you don't compare and compete, everyone will respect you.
47. Having that sense of one's intrinsic worth that constitutes self-respect means potentially having everything.
48. Trust yourself. Every heart vibrates on that iron rope.
49. Make an honest estimate of your abilities, then increase them by ten percent.
50. You ask me what has been my greatest progress? I began to be friends with myself.
51. What you are missing, borrow from yourself.
52. The three most important words you can say to yourself are "Yes, I can!"
53. A person who doubts himself is like a man who wants to join the ranks of the enemy and take up arms against himself. He makes his failure certain since he is the first person to be convinced of it.
54. Your self-esteem is a notch below Kafka's.
55. He is so lacking in self-esteem that the mirror refuses to reflect him.

56. The man who does not appreciate himself cannot value anything or anyone.
57. It begins with unlearning to love others and ends up in not finding in ourselves, anything worthy of being loved.
58. And if our "I" is detestable, loving our neighbor as oneself becomes an atrocious irony.
59. I'm starting to measure myself in strength, not pounds. Sometimes, in smiles.
60. It would be difficult to mention a sign of low self-esteem more certain than the need to perceive another group as inferior.
61. First tell yourself who you want to be; then it does everything accordingly.
62. The most terrifying thing is to accept yourself completely.
63. It takes the devil's work to maintain a good opinion of oneself. Who knows how others do it?
64. When you are able to applaud yourself, it is much easier to applaud others.
65. For some reason, all artists have self-esteem issues.
66. Self- confidence is a strength only until it becomes presumption.

Self-esteem is something difficult to describe, to identify, to analyze, because it is "mobile", it is a function of the past, of the experiences already made, but also of those we are living.

Self-esteem and how to increase it

Feeling worthy of admiration and esteem as well as feeling capable and competent, are indispensable elements of existence. Self-esteem is a "vital" aspect of our psyche. So, let's see how to increase it.

Imagine you are observing an aquarium. Some beautiful, colored fishes swim among the algae, water is their habitat; what is indispensable for their survival. Self-esteem for human beings is like water for fish: It is indispensable for our psychological life because it is responsible for the value that each one recognizes as having as a person. it is a strong motivational boost. Many of our behaviors, from the simplest to the most complex, are aimed at maintaining self-esteem and with it, the image that others will have of us, especially when we fear that this will be jeopardized. How to increase it?

The answers are usually quite counterintuitive. Carl Rogers said:

"Only when I accept myself as I am, I become capable of changing..."

Self-esteem corresponds to the value we give to ourselves as people and to the sense of competence that we recognize in the various areas of our life. It is an aspect of our psychic life that is strongly correlated to identity and to the confirmations we can obtain from others. In fact, each of us is building the foundations for their self-esteem and their sense of identity from childhood. Our parents (first), teachers and other reference adults, have a positive idea of us in mind. They have confidence and appreciation for who we are and what we do.

This way, as we grow and reach adult age, we can internalize this attitude of trust in ourselves and our abilities building an internal source of self-esteem. In adulthood, if our self-esteem is strong enough, it will be less dependent on the need for external confirmation, as opposed to when we were children. We will be able to maintain a sufficiently good image of ourselves despite acknowledged failures, mistakes or shortcomings. However, things are not always so simple. It can happen that in certain circumstances of life, our self-esteem suffers a severe blow. It could also be that one didn't have the opportunity to nurture self-esteem at a young age, resulting in high dependency on the judgment of others, even at an adult age, and consequently, gross insecurity.

Let's dig into what characterizes a fragile self-esteem and how to increase it.

How to raise self-esteem

A rather enlightening joke circulates online about self-esteem and what makes it stable or vulnerable to the judgment of others. A teacher walks into the classroom one day and shows his pupils a 20 dollars ticket, asking them "which of you would like to have it?"

Naturally, everyone raises their hand promptly. Then, the teacher starts crumpling the banknote. When it is all crumpled, he asks his kids "which one of you still wants it?" Again, all hands go up. The teacher throws it on the ground, trampling on it. Afterwards, he asks his students, "Would you still want it?" All hands are raised for the third time.

The teacher then explains to them that, of course, they still want the banknote because, despite being crumpled and trampled on, its value has not changed. In life, he says, many people will make you feel trampled upon or humiliated, but what is important to remember is that your value as a person will not have changed. Self-esteem does not mean having to have something "more", but recognizing what you have and learning to accept yourself as you are. You are already doing well, there is nothing wrong with you, and this is the first step to making your self-esteem more solid. You can really improve yourself.

Strengths and weaknesses

There is an important cognitive distortion that we all commit very often, whenever we feel our self-esteem falter. In psychology, these are called attribution mechanisms, through which we try to give ourselves a plausible explanation for the things that happen to us.

When we do something, we get success or failure (e.g. a university exam, a job interview, etc.) We can attribute the responsibility to ourselves or to the outside (others, luck, chance). If it is true that there are sudden disasters in which there is nothing we can do, it is also true that usually, in most cases, it is possible to identify both an "external" component and a part of our responsibility to the outcome of our actions.

Sometimes it happens that these attributions are too unbalanced. You attribute most of your successes to "luck" or "chance" and you think, are you always most responsible for what is wrong? Probably, your self-esteem would benefit if you can balance things, recognize some merit and be more indulgent with your defects.

Even the opposite mechanism is not healthy for self-esteem. If you are surprised to think that only the merits of your successes go to you and that it is always others who are guilty of what goes wrong, well attention. None of us are omnipotent. Deluding ourselves to be "without error and without blemish" paradoxically makes one's self-esteem much more fragile.

A healthy, solid self-esteem is not based on the conviction of not making mistakes and not having defects, but on the ability to also take responsibility for these most critical aspects of oneself, without decreasing your personal value (20 dollars is still worth 20 dollars...do you remember?)

Ideal Me and Real Me

There is another aspect, always related to attribution mechanisms, which is useful to monitor self-esteem. When we feel that our self-esteem is damaged, we usually feel intense shame and it may happen that a mistake or a failure seems irreparable to us. We may keep hearing that voice, very similar to "what will others think of me now?" Shame, if too pervasive, can be a trap, because it makes us lose the difference between the outcome of our action and the global value of our person.

Even when we happen to make a mistake, it will be good to try to keep these two aspects distinct: The value of a person is not reduced to a single behavior and cannot be questioned by a single failure. "Ideal ego" is an image of how we would like to be, which we try throughout our lives to adapt our "real ego" to.

The discrepancy between these two aspects—how we would like to be and how we really are—can undermine self-esteem and self-image, when we are confronted with an excessively high and unrealistic ideal of ourselves or when, on the contrary, we recognize ourselves lacking ambitions and expectations of improvement about ourselves. The ideals towards which our personality tends must be realistic enough and fantastic enough to serve as a guide and inspiration for the development of ourselves. American actress, Tracee Ellis Ross says: "Every day I strive to make sure that the space between where I am now and where I want to go serves me as inspiration, without frightening me."

How to increase self-esteem (step by step)

*"Self-esteem is what I think about myself.
What I think about myself is determined by
my daily practice. "*

Nothing pompous or superfluous: Self-esteem is the way we see ourselves, and this "lens" can be changed through the actions we perform daily.

Self-esteem is not an innate gift and certainly cannot be magically infused into us by someone or something.

True self-esteem is solid and once it has solidified within us, it cannot be scratched by anything or anyone.

To mold this unshakable confidence in our abilities internally, we need to undertake a journey down a gradual path, a path that may be symbolized with a white staircase.

Each step of this staircase in turn represents a well-defined area of our self-esteem, on which we must intervene.

The scale of self-esteem

Of course, every self-respecting stairway has its own "landing", but I want to focus immediately on the steps, because these are the ones that will allow you to truly believe in yourself, when faced one at a time.

Step # 1 - Listen. The first step to regain our self-esteem involves becoming aware of that little voice that buzzes in our head. Understand when it tells you lies. Silence it or transform it into your ally.

Step # 2 - Accept. The term "accept" immediately makes us think of a passive submission, which isn't the case.

Acceptance, in this case, involves accepting oneself, over and over. This requires a great deal of courage and is the necessary condition to restart.

> *"Only after accepting our limits are we able to overcome them."*

Step # 3 - Face it. When we accept ourselves, we must then take responsibility for what we are experiencing, but also and above all, the responsibility for change.

Step # 4 - Affirm. To increase our self-esteem, we must undoubtedly do important inner work, but we certainly cannot stop there. The next step is to affirm ourselves in the world, or to live in an authentic way, letting our aspirations breathe—expressing ourselves without false masks.

Step # 5 - Take action. Action is the essential ingredient of any path of personal development, but it is not enough to act, it is necessary to act constantly (i.e. with self-discipline) and consistently (i.e. with self-efficacy).

I worked a lot on this path and I took care of every single step down to the smallest detail.

This is written with the aim of accompanying you in the gradual rediscovery of the superhero that resides within you.

It is now up to you to decide whether to look for some palliative to simulate an apparent safety or to undertake with determination, the staircase that stands out in front of you.

Forgive yourself

Forgive yourself - the key to becoming the best version of you

Life is deeply complex. It is made up of events and situations that are often beyond our control. Oftentimes, these events have a decisive impact on who we are, so much so that they prevent us from forgiving ourselves.

-

Anger, resentment, hatred, inferiority, frustration and guilt are so ingrained that we can't help but think about them.

"Many times, hasty decisions, wrong communication or moments of confusion remain inside us like black dots and form part of our soul."

We are often led to reproach ourselves; we blame ourselves when something goes wrong! In doing so, the damage we do ourselves is far greater than what others do.

Forgiveness is by no means an easy path. Forgiving someone for what they have done to us is difficult, and when we have to forgive ourselves for what we have done, this process can be even more complicated. However, by learning to become aware of who we are, by elaborating the dynamics in an objective way, we will be able to forgive ourselves.

There are no people who do not make mistakes

There are mistakes and shortcomings that we just can't forgive ourselves; they cause us anger, remorse and frustration. Just thinking about it, we feel a sense of shame. The only remedy seems to be self-inflicting a just punishment. For some, this can also serve to atone for a fault, as long as it does not last long. But, there comes a day when we need to close the deal with the past and forgive ourselves. Definitely.

The first step to letting go

The simplest way to deal with the most painful feelings is to accept them and let them go. The first step in letting go of what disturbs our balance is being able to find compassion and forgiveness towards ourselves. We all know, however, that we cannot be forced to forgive ourselves.

If we are able to find the courage to open our hearts to ourselves, forgiveness will slowly emerge. How can we begin to approach forgiveness towards ourselves?

Why forgive yourself?

If these feelings of malaise and anger towards ourselves are not attacked from within, we run the risk of adding more and more inches to our emotional armor. Everything we repress poisons us and does nothing but project the exact reflection of the inner world outside. If we look at reality from a hostile perspective, it can only appear hostile to us.

What on earth have you done to be so uncompromising with yourself?

Think you're not a good parent? Know that the perfect parent does not exist! Do you think you are unable to accomplish a goal? Know that life is made up of failures.

Why does everything you do have to turn into a "nothing special"?

"It's nothing, I could have done better."

We often have the ability to belittle everything we do! Are you sure you haven't done anything good in your life? Of course, you can, but if you don't value the things you do, you can never feel worthy of anything. If I asked you to make me a list of all the things you do, you would hardly realize your value—you would say "it's nothing special."

Why do you have to keep living in the past?

All the energy you spend on remembering past mistakes, on reminding yourself of how useless and insignificant you are, you could spend it in putting a stone on everything instead of grounding your life on anger and frustration.

-

5 Affirmations that help you to forgive yourself

Forgiving yourself is not easy and it is not something that can be easily achieved. It is a slow process that requires awareness and change.

1. **I release myself from the heavy burden of doubt, shame and guilt.**

These three emotions are the main cause of many of the problems we face. Forgiving yourself for the actions we have taken or the words we have expressed that have led us to feel shame, guilt or doubt can only improve the quality of our life.

Stopping to analyze the situations that arouse these emotions in us obliges us to recognize our weaknesses. Living this process honestly can only strengthen us emotionally and make us impervious to similar situations in future. It is even possible that we find that what causes us shame, guilt and doubt is, in fact, something of no importance.

2. **I let go of the past to fully experience the future**

At times, all the plans and goals we had were blown up by the past. All those things and people who have harmed us in the past can harm us and prevent us from looking to the future and achieving our goals. To forgive yourself means to stop thinking about everything that is left in the past and cannot be changed.

For example, there are those who do not forgive themselves for not being the right person for someone. We are not perfect and if someone has not found what he was looking for in us, he does not make us worse people.

3. I am able to carry on despite my mistakes

We grew up trying to avoid mistakes and misunderstandings. For this reason, when we feel we have done something wrong, we focus too much on it. We can spend months or years analyzing what went wrong and why.

If we don't start being kind to ourselves, we can never move forward in life. Never forget that we all make mistakes every day and that's okay. We can see every mistake as an experience that has left us something.

Mistakes are the true masters of life. If everything always went well the first time, in a short time, we would be left with no notions to learn, no experiences to talk about or lessons to learn at every mistake. True, there are mistakes that cost us dearly, but even these teach an important lesson.

4. I am grateful for every positive thing that life has given me

Forgiveness also involves realizing and accepting the fact that we are not alone. When we forgive ourselves, all those situations in which we thought it was only our fault, we will see that it is not that difficult to appreciate all the beautiful things that life gives us.

If we make a list right now of the people and things that make our lives better, we will likely find more than we hoped for. When we forgive ourselves for everything, we believe we have caused, it is not that difficult to see all the good in our life.

5. I recognize that I have done everything in my power

If we focus only on the memories or the blame, we give to ourselves, nothing will change. It is better to look to the future and do your best, than live in the regrets of the past. The only one who can truly forgive us is ourselves, by looking in the mirror. The reality is that there are situations in which the only one who can free ourselves from the burden we carry is us.

> *"We are all mixed up with weaknesses and mistakes; let us forgive each other our nonsense: This is the first law of nature."*
>
> Voltaire

We must not forget what we have done in the past but just stop focusing on that. We learn to accept that everyone makes mistakes; only in this way can we take back the command of our life.

We must stop self-pitying and blaming ourselves if we want to regain our right to choose, make mistakes and change!

Forgiveness is difficult. Admitting that there is a problem, and therefore coming to a solution, takes time, patience and courage. When we have to forgive ourselves for what we have done, this process can be even more complicated. Therefore, forgiveness is by no means an easy path. However, by learning to be aware of who you are and to understand that life is a journey, not a race, you too will be able to forgive yourself.

Understand why you need to forgive yourself. When you acknowledge that you've made a mistake, you may feel guilty and need to forgive yourself. In these cases, memories of the past could give you this sense of discomfort. To find the source of these feelings, ask yourself:

Do I feel this way because the consequences of my behavior make me feel bad?

Why am I to blame for what has happened negative?

Accept that failures don't make you a bad person. Everyone can make mistakes in life. Don't think that by failing at something—whether it's a job or a relationship—you become a bad person. As Bill Gates said: "It's okay to celebrate success, but it's more important to pay attention to the lessons we learn when we make mistakes."

Learning from your mistakes is the first step in being able to forgive yourself.

Don't be afraid to start over. To be able to forgive yourself, you don't have to be afraid of starting from scratch. Learning to grant yourself forgiveness does not only mean learning to live with your past, but to treasure experiences. Therefore, take what you have learned and apply it in your life to improve yourself.

Adopt a new mindset by learning from the wrongs of the past. One way to move on is to smooth out some aspects of your character, based on what your life experiences have taught you.

Set goals for the future that will help improve your thinking and make it stronger. Such a look into the future will allow you to forgive yourself today and focus on the positive changes you are able to make.

When you feel guilty, remember Les Brown's words: "Forgive your flaws and mistakes, then move on." They will help you whenever you make a mistake.

Leave the past behind you

Realize that no one is perfect. You should forgive yourself even if you have behaved badly towards someone else. First, keep in mind that you have nothing to blame for the actions of others. We all make mistakes and go through moments in life when we don't behave well. If you become aware of this, you will take the first step that will lead you to improve.

Don't dwell on the mistakes of the past. It helps to treasure it, but if you linger too long, you won't be able to forgive yourself. This attitude may prevent you from being aware of the present. You may find yourself in an impasse and find that you are obsessed with what you did or didn't do. Instead, focus on the present and how you can take action in the future to improve your life.

Plan a bright future today so you don't get stifled by the past. Consider taking an approach to life that leads you to "solve problems and move on." If an encounter painfully relives something that happened in the past, focus on what you can control.

Try to solve the problems you know you can handle and try to let go of everything else. You shouldn't keep repeating the same mistakes.

Learn to be aware. Being aware of your actions can help you recover. If you have a strong sense of self and carry out everything you decide to do, with knowledge of the facts, you have the opportunity to build a better future and forgive yourself for attitudes or reactions you displayed in the past.

Analyze your past decisions. It is not wise to dwell on mistakes, but you have to learn from mistakes to move forward in the healthiest way.

One way to forgive yourself is to identify the factors, or causes, from which emotions arise. If you can understand how you have behaved from the start, then you can change your perspective on the future.

Ask yourself:

> *"What did I do the first time and what can I do now to prevent the same result from happening?"*

Recognize situations in which you feel strong emotions. This way, you will be able to clearly identify the circumstances in which you feel uncomfortable. Once the situation is identified, it will be easier to plan a solution. Ask yourself:

Do I feel anxious or guilty when I approach my boss?

Do I experience strong negative emotions when talking to my partner?

Does being together with my parents make me feel angry or nervous?

Show forgiveness to yourself and others

Welcome the people into your life.

As the philosopher Derrida once said: "Forgiveness is often confused with similar aspects, sometimes in a calculated way: Apologies, regrets, amnesty, prescription, etc."

Forgiveness is a two-way street. You probably won't come to forgive yourself if you don't learn to forgive others. Therefore, you shouldn't chase people out of your life if you want to have all the support you need to grant yourself forgiveness.

Talk to the people you love to find support as you go out of your way to forgive yourself.

Come up with a solution or plan.

To absolve yourself of something, you must be aware of the mistakes to be forgiven. By writing a precise plan down to the smallest detail, you will be able to reflect on what is important and have an orderly set of mistakes, for which you must apologize to yourself or someone else. [9] Take the following into consideration when looking for a solution to ask for forgiveness:

Affirm or apologize using direct language. Don't go around the problem. Try saying directly, "I'm sorry" or "Forgive me?" You shouldn't be ambiguous or false.

Try to figure out how you can actually find a solution. If you are going to apologize to someone, think about actions that can help you remedy the situation. If forgiveness is about yourself, ask yourself what steps you need to take to move forward in life wisely.

Promise yourself and others that you will do everything to perform better in the future. It makes no sense to apologize if words are not followed by actions. Make sure you don't repeat the same mistakes.

Apologize to people.

If you ask them for forgiveness, you will feel better about yourself.

Sometimes, by clarifying the situation, it is possible to solve a problem. This will also give you the opportunity to make it clear that in your eyes the problem had taken on greater proportions than it actually was. [10] It has been shown that asking for forgiveness can lead to more positive results and stronger relationships.

Take Responsibility for Your Actions

Be honest with yourself about your behavior.

Before you can fully forgive, you need to acknowledge what you have done.

It may be helpful to write down the actions that cause strong feelings. By doing this, you will be able to identify concrete examples of why you have negative feelings about yourself.

Stop rationalizing and start taking responsibility for what you say and do. **One way to be honest with yourself is to accept the consequences of your actions. If you have said or done something wrong, you need to take responsibility for your behavior before granting yourself forgiveness.**

One way to achieve this is to get rid of stress. The more you hold it, the more damage you will do to yourself.

Stress can sometimes cause you to release pent-up anger and harm yourself as much as the people around you, but if you forgive yourself, the anger will disappear, and with it all negative things. As a result, you will be more focused and better prepared to view reality positively, rather than negatively.

Accept the guilt you feel.

Accepting responsibility for one's actions is one thing, but understanding the emotions that accompany them is another. Feeling strong emotions, such as guilt, is not only a common experience for everyone, but also good. The sense of guilt, in fact, encourages you to work for yourself and others.

You may feel guilty about what you think. You have likely wished people pain or misfortune at times or felt a desire to satisfy some carnal pleasure or your greed.

If you are plagued by these feelings of guilt, know that they are quite common. Yours can also depend on strong emotions. Therefore, it's best to face them and recognize why you feel this way. Only in this way will you be able to forgive yourself.

Probably because of your guilt feelings, you will judge yourself (or you will judge others) very severely. You could dump what you feel on yourself and other people or you could accuse them of your insecurities, exacerbating your feelings of guilt.

If you find yourself accusing someone, take a step back and try to figure out why. It could be helpful on your path of self-forgiveness.

You may feel guilty about someone else's behavior. It is not uncommon for a couple to experience this feeling due to their partner's conduct. Therefore, you may feel responsible for the actions or insecurities of those around you.

You need to identify the regions you feel this way for so you can see if you need to forgive yourself or another person.

Recognize your values and principles.

Before granting yourself forgiveness, you must identify the things that have a certain meaning to you, in which you believe. Think for a moment about how you might remedy the behaviors you feel guilty about and how you might change the situation. The way you act could be based on a system of religious or cultural beliefs.

Analyze your needs versus your desires.

When you feel a sense of inadequacy, one way to forgive yourself is to understand what you feel is necessary in your life, in relation to what you want.

Determine what your most concrete needs are—such as a home, food and social needs—and compare them with what you crave most: A nicer car, a bigger house, a better physique. By identifying your needs in relation to your desires, you will realize that perhaps you have been too hard on yourself or that perhaps you cannot control every aspect of reality.

Test yourself to do good

Become a better person by setting personal challenges for yourself. In order not to find yourself in a situation of doubt and guilt, put in place, small challenges that allow you to improve personally.

You can do this by developing a monthly schedule that covers an aspect you want to improve. By committing to something for a month—for example, keeping track of your calorie consumption—you will begin to acquire habits that will lead you to progress. You will come to forgive yourself through constructive attitudes.

Work on any flaws you've noticed you have. Try to make a personal assessment to understand the tools you need to improve.

For example, if you feel guilty about putting off something, make a to-do list and try to respect it. It is important to identify the aspects that are under your control.

This exercise will allow you to forgive yourself through personal progress.

Become aware of yourself.

Self-awareness is the ability to predict the consequences of one's actions. By reflecting on yourself and your actions, you will be able to become a better person while setting moral rules for yourself. You can come to this realization by highlighting your strengths, observing your reactions to situations and expressing the emotions you feel.

Advice

Instead of thinking about the past, *focus on the present and prepare for the future*. Remember not to lock yourself in the past! You are a fantastic and beautiful person! Learn from your mistakes, forgive yourself and move on!

Think about how you have forgiven others in the past. Take advantage of these experiences and apply what you have learned in various situations in life. The reassuring aspect is that you know you have the ability to forgive, so you just have to channel it in the right direction.

The mistakes of the past have most likely made you the person you are today. So, don't consider them as simple mistakes, but as life lessons.

The mistakes you make don't define who you are. Believe in the fact that you are a wonderful person. Think of all the monstrous mistakes made by normal or good people and from whom they have learned. You will find that yours aren't that bad!

The people we are is the result of the good and bad things that happen to us in life, as well as the good and bad things we have done.

How we react to negative events is as important as how we react to happier ones. A person who tends to mull over and overstate a bad event will be more likely to live with anger and resentment and expect a negative future, than someone who sees pitfalls as isolated incidents that do not affect their way of being.

Forgiving yourself and others do not mean forgetting the past. It means canceling all resentment within oneself, even if the memory remains. It is comparable to grieving.

Life goes on, so forgive and forget.

Forgive anyone who does you wrong and, hopefully in the future, they will understand that their actions were wrong, reconciling with both you and themselves. Go on because life is too precious to be lived in bitterness.

Get a stress reliever. When you start to feel guilty, use it.

Another great way to forgive yourself is to help others. By doing so, you will feel so much compassion for them that you will clear your guilt. Remember not to think about the mistakes you have made, because life is too short to be lived with pain.

Warnings

Don't hang out with people who recall your past in a negative way. Get away from all those who irritate you, underestimate you or belittle you and who do not consider your vulnerability.

Avoid talking about your mistakes and putting yourself in a bad light with other people. They will be convinced too. Go to therapy to get these negative thoughts out of your mind and stop being swayed.

Stay away from people who keep you from improving. Most of the time, they are focused on their insecurities and see those who manage to overcome the hostilities of life as a threat. Accept the fact that in some cases, by forgiving yourself, you risk losing some relationship where negativity was a source of power the other person exercised over you. Ask yourself if you'd rather continue to have an unhappy relationship or move on to become a new person, who is capable of establishing healthier relationships.

Knowing how to forgive is a very difficult quality to cultivate, but one of the most important. By learning to forgive both yourself and others, you will take a big step forward in your personal growth—a reward that will repay you for all your efforts.

-

PROTECT AND TAKE CARE OF YOURSELF

HOW TO BE HAPPY IN LIFE ALONE

"Take care of your thoughts; they will become words.

Take care of your words; they will become actions.

Take care of your actions; they will become habits.

Take care of your habits; they will become the character.

Take care of your character; it will become your destiny. "

- Ralph Waldo Emerson

The concept behind this thought, generalizing and simplifying to a minimum, is the consideration "okay, let's help others, do good, but let's not be fooled, let's not let others put their feet in our head." I have thought for a long time on this type of considerations and I take advantage of this post to express my point of view on it. I simply believe, in general terms, that our needs and interests should not be contrasted with the needs and interests of those around us.

Overcoming shame, healing trauma.

Beyond fear and insecurity, regain love for yourself. In short, I am of the opinion that one should not cancel one's needs behind the noble objective of giving oneself to others. Above all, I believe that loving each other and taking care of ourselves at 360 degrees constitute the fundamental and essential prerequisite for being able to dedicate ourselves to others, help them grow as individuals and offer them kindness, compassion and love.

If we are not well, how could we ever imagine being able to make others happy? To be able to represent an added value for others, we must therefore first demonstrate love for ourselves.

From today:

START TAKING CARE OF YOUR HAPPINESS

Many of us spend our days unhappy and discontented, but at the same time, we do little to change the status quo. Instead, try to make your happiness a goal to focus on. Make sure that your every action, your every gesture and your every word are in line with YOUR idea of happiness. Work for your well-being, take responsibility for it, and don't let others decide who and what can make you happy.

START TAKING CARE OF YOUR THOUGHTS

Don't let negative thoughts prevail in your mind. Make room for your positivity. Strive to always observe reality from a confident and optimistic perspective, striving under all circumstances to consciously formulate positive and constructive thoughts. Don't ignore your thoughts: Observe them, become aware of them and let the negative thoughts go away, without allowing them to envelop you in their pessimistic spiral.

START TAKING CARE OF YOUR UNIQUENESS

Your strengths and weaknesses make you a unique and extraordinary being. You don't need to look like anyone else, you are already perfect as you are. Be inspired by the people you admire, never stop improving yourself, but always remember to value what makes you exceptional: Your uniqueness. Never think that you are wrong or that you have something less than those around you. There is no one like you. You are unique, perfect and extraordinary.

START TAKING CARE OF YOUR EMOTIONS

When we become prey to emotions that we can hardly control (e.g. crying, anger, anxiety), in retrospect, we often tend to judge ourselves negatively, condemning ourselves. We consider ourselves weak and "wrong", we feel guilty and different from how we should be.

But, this is not the case. Don't judge your emotions. Observe them and accept them with awareness, without condemnation. Your emotions reflect your essence, your personality and your innermost needs. Don't judge them, don't condemn them, but take care of them.

START TAKING CARE OF YOUR DREAMS

Someone said that the world belongs to those who believe in the beauty of their dreams. I believe that dreams represent the real engine of our existence. I believe dreams do not exist to be analyzed or dissected too deeply, to be judged or even condemned. Dreams exist to be lived. No one else can decide what our dreams are, apart from us. Dreams are thrill, enthusiasm, emotions. Dreams are pure energy. Look after them and never stop chasing them.

CHAPTER 2: Useful Tips

Taking care of yourself is the basis of your physical and mental well-being; we cannot think of finding a balance without self-love. Taking care of yourself is a fundamental gesture and is not based only on taking care of your physical appearance. It is mainly based on the love you feel towards you.

When we say we take care of ourselves, we don't always know exactly what we are talking about and we risk losing the fundamental points of this way of life.

Deciding to love yourself, take care of your mind and body is a real lifestyle that can only enrich your life. How can you start this new path?

Let's see the best tips to start taking care of yourself.

Train and meditate

Keeping your body toned and active is one of the best ways to start the day right. Another very important tip is to take time to meditate. Use some of your time to reflect and relax, dedicate that hour to yourself and forget all the stresses. Besides meditation, exercising regularly is another very good tip that everyone should follow. Our body needs stimulation. The endorphins released by sporting activity will only put you in a good mood and improve your day. Deciding to play a sport helps you understand how far you can go, encourages you to give your best, makes you believe in yourself and in your potential.

By practicing a sport and keeping fit you will get very good results. You will be able to love your body more every day and welcome new challenges. Only you can choose what to do and how to approach physical activity. Always remember that it is your choice and must make you happy. Sport must always be a pleasant moment, never a constraint. If you need to download energy at the end of the day, you could try a martial art. If you need to lose weight, you could devote yourself to an activity that involves a high intensity workout. Once you find your routine, you will understand why moving is so good, especially mentally.

Read, study and inform yourself

Loving yourself also means taking care of your intellect and curiosity. Be curious. Try to learn something new every day. Read, study and find out about something that really interests you. Wanting to enrich yourself with new information is an absolutely positive and productive thing. You will keep your mind active; you will understand new things and you will be able to relate to different people based on the nature of topic you choose.

Our heads always need stimulation to be happy. Have you ever noticed that spending hours and hours on social networks makes you more dissatisfied than reading a good book? Reading stimulates you. It makes your imagination fly. Reading enriches you and makes you feel good. Your mind needs to be pampered with good books, with interesting information, it needs to feel active and not passive. A very important tip is to always keep a high level of curiosity, learn to be more curious if you are not already curious. Why is being curious important in loving yourself? This is because, through curiosity and the desire to discover something new, will you be able to look at the world with positive eyes always. Positivity is the basis of your self-love and the desire to take care of your soul. Don't get bored. Be lively and curious and you will see that your mood will always be high!

Surround yourself with positivity

It will seem trivial but it is not. Surrounding ourselves with people who give us something positive is a choice that we have to make at some point in our life. Taking care of ourselves also means knowing how to push away someone or something that doesn't make us feel good. Try to do an action every day that gives you some positivity and a good mood. Avoid people who try to suck your energy and opt for those who make you smile. Many times, it is difficult to realize that a person is not good for us, the sensations in these cases are the best answer.

The most recurrent sensations we can experience when we are not comfortable are:

- Feeling inferior to that person;
- Discomfort in being next to us;
- Inability to express yourself in his presence;
- Fear of being judged;
- Feeling of being laughed at or otherwise treated as if you were worth little.

All these emotions are not the fruit of your imagination, they are signals. If you feel like this when you are in the presence of someone, then it is time to take action and Change Company, friends, acquaintances and environment. Loving and taking care of yourself also means this: Knowing how to dose your time and give it only to those who give us positivity. Those who undermine your self-esteem will NEVER help you live well, and it is important that you understand this as soon as possible. Only in this way can you truly take care of yourself and love yourself.

Create a healthy and balanced routine

Creating a routine is very important to feel good and take care of yourself.

Make sense of your day and set it up according to this pattern:

- Eat in a healthy and balanced way.
- Drink a lot of water, perhaps with lemon inside, if you can avoid caffeine do so.
- Exercise, take care of your body.
- Organize the study\ work by schematizing deadlines and timelines. This way, you will avoid anxiety and fear of not succeeding.
- Talk to someone you love every day and avoid those who make you feel bad.
- Meditate and relax before going to sleep, it will help your night rest and you will feel better.
- Read something interesting, paint, draw or write, use your head and creativity in free moments and be active.
- Focus on what your short and long-term goals are. Live every day trying to reach your goal and stay positive.
- Do not look at others, do not criticize them and do not throw out negativity. Use these energies to focus on yourself.

It is important to create a routine like this, in order to have balance in your life. Taking care of yourself also means knowing how to manage your time and not throw it away! Have you ever seen someone inspiring spending hours and hours on the couch watching TV? I do not believe. Those who love themselves and those who care about being well, face the days as if they always had something to learn. This is what you have to do if you really love yourself. Study, improve yourself, and try to reach your goals. This is the key to taking care of yourself both externally and internally.

A person who does not know himself cannot love himself fully.

Get to know yourself, learn what you want and where you want to go. Once you understand all these things, take action. The importance of taking care of yourself is so great that you can't waste even a minute. If you haven't done so until today, tomorrow is the right day to start.

Take a diary, write down your daily routine, introduce everything you did not know and everything you would like to be part of your day. Remember to put the things you need to do first, learn to manage them in the right way! Give yourself breaks and rewards, you will see that it will be easier to finish a day of work.

-

Conclusion: Love and take care of yourself

The ones we have listed are the basic tips for starting a journey of personal growth.

By personal growth, we mean all the positive aspects that can contribute to your realization. In a nutshell, heal yourself in 360 degrees.

Taking care of yourself doesn't mean always having perfect hair or a trendy coat. Taking care of yourself means aiming for improvement day after day. All this happens thanks to a process of personal growth—an important and necessary process to make you understand who you are and where you want to go in your life.

Don't waste time and roll up your sleeves. Start taking care of yourself! Loving yourself also means knowing how to use grit in the right moments, getting up after a failure and having tenacity to try again, until your goals are successful.

Respect yourself and treat you better

12 phrases you must be able to say to yourself every day

1. "I AM FOLLOWING MY HEART AND MY INTUITION."

Don't get carried away by your problems. Be guided by your dreams. Live the life you want to live. Make your own decisions and act on them.

Make mistakes, fall and try again. Even if you fall a thousand times, you will still have the awareness that you have given your all to make your dreams come true.

Our hearts burn for something: It is our job to keep this fire alive and well fed. This is your life, and it's short. Don't let others put out the flame.

Try what you want to try. Go where you want to go. Follow your intuition.

Visualize your dream. Every day, try to take one small step to make it come true.

As you strive to achieve your goals, you may run into some disappointments along the way.

Don't be discouraged. Think of these disappointments as challenges, tests of persistence and courage. At the end of the road, most of the time, you will look at failures and disappointments with a big smile.

2. "I AM PROUD OF MYSELF."

You are your best friend and your most severe critic.

Regardless of the opinions of others, at the end of the day, the person you have to deal with is only you.

Constantly strive to improve yourself, but accept and love yourself for the wonderful person you already are.

Visualize the person you would like to become and give your best to achieve this.

Being proud of yourself doesn't mean bragging about how great you are, but appreciating yourself for who you are and striving to become an even better person.

You are not perfect, but you deserve to be loved.

All you have to do is live a story that no one else can ever live in your place: The story of your life.

3. "I AM HAVING A POSITIVE IMPACT ON THE LIVES OF OTHERS".

In your every gesture, in your every word, you act with the aim of making a difference in the lives of others.

Always try to have a positive impact on others.

It is by helping others that we can fulfill our destiny.

When we manage to make the existence of others even a little bit better, it means that our life is also benefiting from it.

Make your actions go beyond yourself and help others be happier or suffer less.

You have your own extraordinary individuality, but you are part of a wonderful whole.

You can't always solve every difficult situation, but you can always do something for others.

Sometimes, a sincere smile is enough to brighten another person's life.

4. "I AM HAPPY AND GRATEFUL."

Happiness is within you, in your way of thinking and in the perspective through which you decide to observe the reality that surrounds you.

The way you look at yourself and the world is the result of a choice and the unconscious habit of continuing to follow up on that choice.

The lens through which you choose to view reality determines how you feel, your mood and as well as the difference between happiness and unhappiness.

Being grateful for what you have is a great way to welcome happiness inside of you.

Whenever you feel down, review all that is wonderful in your life. You will feel pervaded by the clear feeling that you are a lucky person and that you have many very good reasons to be happy.

5. "I AM MYSELF."

Judy Garland once said, "Always be the original version of yourself, rather than someone else's draft."

Try to shape your life on this statement.

You cannot live someone else's life. The only shoes in which you can give your best are yours.

If you are not yourself, you are not truly living. You are merely existing. Trying to be someone else is a waste of energy.

Embrace and the wonderful individual within you. Embrace and welcome your ideas, dreams, passions and goals.

Always try to be yourself—the best version of yourself, on your terms.

Continuously improve, take care of your body and health, and surround yourself with positivity.

6. "I LIVE FULL OF THE TIME I HAVE AVAILABLE."

Time is one of the most precious components of your life.

Regardless of what you are doing, even when you are just lazing around, try to be truly present in the moment.

Find the passion in your life, discover the world and travel, or just observe the world that is around you right now. Hang out with great people, do amazing things, eat amazing food and savor the little pleasures in life.

Remember that time is precious, but it's free. You can't own it, but you can use it. You can spend it, but you can't keep it.

Let your dreams be bigger than your fears and your actions stronger than your words.

7. "I AM HONEST WITH MYSELF."

Always try to be honest with yourself about what's right and what's wrong, based on your values.

Be honest about the goals you want to achieve and the person you want to become.

Always be honest with yourself and every aspect of your life.

You are the only person you really have to deal with every day.

8. "I AM CLOSE TO THOSE I LOVE."

Distance in relationships is not measured by distance, but by the intensity of feelings.

Our loved ones can be hundreds of miles apart, but the relationship will still work great if we are able to make our closeness felt to those we love.

So, don't neglect the people you care about, because lack of attention often hurts more than words spoken in anger.

Stay in touch with those who are important to you. When was the last time you told a family member or partner that you love them?

Simple demonstrations of affection are enough to make someone understand how much you care.

Talk to the people you love, give them your time, listen to them and let them know that you are there.

Create your destiny.

9. "I KNOW WHAT IT MEANS TO LOVE UNCONDITIONALLY."

Whether your love is towards a child, a partner, or another family member, it is wonderful to know the feeling of giving love while expecting nothing in return. This is unconditional love.

An existence lived under the sign of unconditional love is an extraordinary adventure that excites the heart and illuminates our path.

This love is that dynamic and powerful energy that lifts us up in the most difficult moments.

When you love unconditionally, it is not because the person you love is perfect, but because you learn to love them for the extraordinary creature that they are, with all their wonderful strengths and fantastic flaws.

10. "I HAVE FORGIVEN THOSE WHO HAVE HURT ME".

Each of us, at some point in our life, has been hurt by another person. We have been treated badly, our trust has broken down, we have suffered.

If it is true that this pain is normal, it is also true that sometimes this pain lingers for too long. We relive it indefinitely and carry it with us, instead of doing everything to get rid of it.

Enter the perspective that the past is gone. Treasure the teachings that life has given you and look to the future with confidence and renewed spirit.

Grudges are a perfect waste of happiness, which makes us miss the opportunity to admire the beauty of existence.

Forgiveness is like freeing a prisoner and discovering that that prisoner was you.

11. "I TAKE FULL RESPONSIBILITY FOR MY LIFE."

Take full responsibility for your choices and mistakes, and be prepared to do whatever it takes to make the right decisions and remedy the mistakes you've made.

Either you take full responsibility for your life or someone else will do it for you.

When that happens, you will become a slave to the ideas and dreams of others, rather than the architect of your own life. You are the only person who can directly control the outcome of your life. It won't always be easy. Each person has a mountain of obstacles to climb.

Taking responsibility for your life means deciding to do what is necessary to overcome these obstacles.

Don't just survive, thrive.

12. "I HAVE NO REGRETS."

This is simply the culmination of the previous eleven points. Follow your heart. Be true to yourself. Do what makes you happy.

Stay with whoever makes you smile. Laugh as much as you can. Love as much as you can.

Say what you feel the need to say. Help out when you are able to. Appreciate everything you have. Smile. Celebrate your little wins.

Learn from your mistakes. Forgive and let go of the things you can't control.

CHAPTER 3: View Life on a Positive Side as a Single

Living alone will significantly improve your life

Living alone brings several benefits, which is why nowadays, more and more people choose to adopt this "lone wolf" or "free spirit" lifestyle, and prefer living together with themselves rather than with other people.

Although loneliness is generally frowned upon, it can teach you a lot about yourself. It can make you stronger, give you a better understanding of yourself, and improve your relationships with others, as demonstrated by these 10 benefits you will gain by choosing to live alone.

Loneliness is no longer synonymous with isolation. Renewal science is finally on the side of those who prefer to live alone.

Sociologist Eric Klinenberg explains in his book Going Solo: The *Straordinary Rise and Surprising Appeal of Living Alone*, how "loneliness has the ability to be liberating and soothing." He also states: "Compared to married couples, people who live alone are more likely to go out to restaurants, play sports, go to exhibitions, go to the cinema or engage in associations." Furthermore, a University of Michigan study shows that the bad mood of those who share our life could have negative effects on us.

-

10 more reasons why living alone is just great:

1- You begin to understand your skills

If you've never lived alone, it might seem strange to you. Yet, living alone teaches you how to manage and use your skills. While it's not easy, over time, you will be able to do a lot more things than you thought. If you've had trouble asking for help in the past, you'll learn how to do it and when it's needed, which is a good thing.

2- Optimize your decision-making skills

If you are in the habit of being in a relationship, you may not be used to making decisions on your own, but when you live alone, you can do it without having to be judged for your choices. It is difficult to adapt initially, especially when you are used to following another person's advice, but you will end up finding it very pleasant.

3- It makes you start discovering yourself

Living alone provides an ideal solitary environment to learn more about ourselves, our strengths, our weaknesses, our desires, our motivations, our behaviors—without distractions. Living alone gives us more time to focus on ourselves and helps us develop our skills for introspection.

4- It helps you to improve your creativity

Living alone gives you the time and freedom to explore and work on your passions. Most of the great writers, artists and musicians have connected to their creativity in solitude, which offers the best environment to think, dream and create.

5- It relieves you of some responsibilities

You can do what you want, when you want and where you want, when you live alone. You don't have the weight and pressure of having to do constant and boring chores and duties. While living with other people involves sharing some duties, you will enjoy having nothing to do with anyone.

6- It helps you to evacuate the pressure of work

Living alone gives you complete freedom to relax and unwind, so you can feel comfortable even on the busiest days. This is particularly useful for empathic and extremely sensitive people, who often carry the weight of the confidences they have received during the day, which influence them.

7- It makes you appreciate others more

Living alone creates a harmonious balance in your life, which allows you to appreciate and value the presence of others more. Human nature prompts us to take friends, family and loved ones for granted, but living alone, without the presence of others, reminds us of their true value.

8- It gives you a sense of personal pride

When you live alone, you learn to take care of yourself, because you know no one else will. You know that you are the main actor in your life and you respect yourself. Also, you will be proud to live alone and take care of yourself.

9- It helps you to manage your money better

One of the main benefits of living alone is achieving true financial independence. People living alone cannot rely on their roommates or parents to pay their rent or bills. This quickly teaches you to master your finances—a skill that will be useful to you throughout your life.

10- If you are introverted, you will like it

For introverted people, it's the best life they can live. They will have as much time alone as they want. Not having to surround yourself with people, at least when you really don't want to, is a very rewarding thing if you are that type of person.

15 reasons why you should live alone at least once in your life

Do you feel lonely sometimes? Sure. But, many find beauty in absolute solitude.

There are those who tremble at the thought of living alone. Yet, those who have really tried it say that the experience was not only pleasant, but also formative.

1. You dictate the house rules.

Living alone means that I can be the master of my zen, at any time. If I want calm and silence, I can have them. If I want to improvise a dance party in the kitchen, no problem. If I want to sleep until ten on Sunday or get up early to do yoga, I do. If I want to leave dirty dishes in the sink, ditto. If I want to spend three straight hours cleaning the baseboards, well, I can do that too. If I just want to sit and read a book with the dogs crouched at my feet, same story. Living alone for me means having the freedom to cultivate a home environment that recharges my soul.

2. You get to know yourself better

It's the best way to get to know yourself, but it takes courage. There's no one to "distract" you from building your life, make decisions for you, or fix things you don't want to worry about. After a while, you will find that you are the only person you need, and the madness of life doesn't seem so scary anymore.

3. For an introvert it's a dream come true...

I enjoy peace and silence alone; pure bliss. I am accepting my introverted nature; I can stay alone at home without being judged for not being sociable. I can get into bed at 6:30 in the dark of winter evenings and nobody cares. It is fantastic.

4. ...but also, for an extrovert.

As an extrovert, who draws her energy from contact with others, I didn't think I would like to live alone. Instead, I loved it! I learned to meditate! It made me realize how much I really enjoy having time, all to myself.

5. You will face some of your fears.

You have to be brave to deal with strange and frightening noises, or to be the only one who goes to open the door. You have to take care of bills and security. You will be the one to deal with the disturbing insects and you will understand when to ask for help.

6. You will become aware of your abilities.

I frankly believe that everyone should live alone for at least a couple of years. No roommates, relatives or friends—alone. Pay your bills on time, learn from the consequences of failing to manage your budget, suffer fever and chills with no one to take care of them but you. Living alone hardens your character.

7. You will be more comfortable with yourself.

I realized that I loved living alone. If I hadn't learned to be with myself and enjoy my own company, who would have liked it? It was liberating, peaceful and formative. Looking back, I am grateful for that experience.

8. You can monopolize the bed.

The bed is all mine and I don't have to share an inch. I was able to understand what I want, what I need and how to take care of who I am.

9. You can decorate the room according to your preferences.

I painted the walls with the brightest colors— orange, pink, mint, blue—and embellished them with prints and photos that I like. Prior to living alone, I had never been able to decorate a space exactly the way I wanted.

10. You don't have to compromise when your lifestyle is at stake.

I miss living alone. I have been living with my boyfriend for five years in a small apartment in San Francisco. I can work all day and have a successful career, but I have to recharge in the evening. And now, when I get home, there is not only one person to relate to, which takes energy, but there are also compromises! Lots of compromises! Like preparing a real dinner. I could eat cereal for dinner. I can no longer decide that maybe it's one of those days when I just want to go home, put on my pajamas and fall asleep on the couch at seven in the evening. Even when I try, he wakes me up for bed. What courage!

11. You don't have to worry about your roommate making a mess or using your stuff without asking your permission.

I can fix everything and clean up before I go to work and, when I get back, everything is in its place. It's easier to prepare and portion the food you always find there in the fridge, where you left it. Plus, hosting people, organizing parties and sleepovers without having to coordinate with roommates is great.

12. It can make you even more productive.

I realized that there is a distinct difference between loneliness and being lonely. Sometimes, I feel like going out, but no one is available, so I feel "alone", then I look around and see laundry and dirty dishes. I decided to be productive and be enough for myself. In that moment, I'm happy with my loneliness.

13. You are free to sing out loud, dance or walk around the house naked if you like.

I can sing until I lose my voice and nobody notices (the dog may bark because I suck, but nothing more). It is the place where I can truly be myself, alone, on my terms.

14. Encourages you to make an extra effort to see friends.

It's all too easy to stay at home and spend time alone, but I've learned to communicate more with others and to further cultivate my friendships.

15. You gain confidence because you know that you will be fine on your own no matter what.

I have lived most of my life making sure everyone around me was okay, and living alone has taught me to worry about my well-being too. At twenty-four, I realized that I purposely avoided relationships for fear of feeling constrained and dependent on others. I was afraid of finding myself in a toxic relationship and feeling stuck, unable to escape. After trying it, and realizing that I can do it and that I like it, living alone is ALWAYS a viable option for me. I no longer have to fear vulnerability, because now I know what independence is and I can open up to relationships.

That's why, according to science, living alone is better

Do you have to be with someone to be happy?

Apparently not, even alone you are fine. Indeed, according to science, those who live alone are much better off than those who live together.

Living alone, in fact, offers the opportunity to continually renew.

According to Klinenberg,

"loneliness has the ability to make us feel free and relaxed. Compared to those who live with their partner, those who live alone

> *are more inclined to go to restaurants, to play sports, to go to exhibitions, to the cinema and to engage in social work".*

Those who live with their partner have many more constraints and are not free to do what they want, when they want.

To confirm this thesis, there is also a recent study from the University of Michigan, which showed how living with another person affects health. For example, living with someone who is often in a bad mood has negative effects on mental health.

Living alone, on the other hand, has several advantages. First of all, it helps to become autonomous and to have more confidence in oneself and abilities. You focus much more on your needs and don't have to put them aside to make someone else happy. Finally, the most obvious thing: At home, you are completely free to do what you want, how you want to do it, to come and go at any time and bring in new friends...even in the bedroom!

In the course of our lives, there always comes a time when we are forced, in one way or another, to leave our family nest, either as a necessity or for personal growth. The thing I am sure of, however, is that before running into another cohabitation, be it with friends, boyfriends or strangers, it would be better to first learn to live alone. I think that in order to live well with other people, you must first be able to feel good about yourself. Indeed, how can we expect to share and have a happy and balanced life with a person, if before we have not been able to build solid foundations for a peaceful coexistence with ourselves?

The idea of living alone probably scares you and I'm sure that a lot of doubts and questions are already blending into your head. Are you wondering if you are able to live alone? Not sure which is the best choice? Not sure if you are strong enough to face your fears and insecurities? Today, I will help you face this new situation, providing you with answers and useful advice to your questions and anxieties as much as possible.

Moving and becoming independent have always been difficult actions, full of obstacles and anxieties. The latter were then exacerbated and aggravated during this year 2020, due to the Covid-19 pandemic, surprising many to have to face a quarantine in solitude.

Are you alone due to the sudden departure of your roommates, who have decided to return to their family? Did you decide from the beginning to live just to be free and away from a possible intrusive roommate? No matter the reason for your loneliness, now you will probably feel lost and distressed at the idea of the next few weeks that await you and you will surely be wondering what to do.

Before throwing yourself into any hasty conclusion, perhaps dictated by the anxiety of the moment, you should think and ask yourself questions: Does returning home involve a risk for you and your family? Is it still possible to return? Are you ready to go back to sharing your spaces 24/7 with your family? Are you ready to change your habits again?

Unless there is a real need, perhaps related to your family's health issues, you may try to see the situation as a challenge to grow and become even more independent and strong. On the other hand, I imagine that one of the main reasons that led you to break away from mom and dad was the desire to achieve total independence and the desired freedom. This is the best situation to be able to show them your maturity and strength in dealing with the problems that come your way in difficult times like this. It will be a great opportunity to show yourself your skills too!

Too much is good! How to manage too much free time?

In a normal situation, having too much free time would not be considered a headache. Indeed, especially in big cities, our real problem would seem to be the exact opposite—the lack of time! In fact, during the day, we have a lot of things to do, from work, to study, to various commitments with family and friends. So, we're not really used to having to manage such an abundance of free time. Now, you're probably wondering: What can I do all day at home alone? How can I manage all this time if I live alone?

Take a few breaths and relax, because below, I have collected for you, a series of practical tips on how to manage this new and unexpected situation.

7 tips to better manage too much free time when living quarantine alone

Break up your love affair with the bed. In situations of boredom and loneliness, the bed represents our little corner of paradise, but we must know how to say no to this toxic love! Also, lying down for too long causes the muscles and some internal organs to become lazy, causing them to lose their tone, thus becoming less reactive and less efficient.

Give a time limit to Netflix time and social time. Like everything else, you need to know how to control yourself. Using the telephone, TV and computer too much not only hurt because of the radiation to which you are exposed, but also makes you addicted.

Say stop binging against boredom. We know that food is one of our few joys in life, especially in times of high stress or loneliness, but you need to be strong enough to be able to say no. The question must be asked: Am I really hungry or am I just bored?

Maintain a healthy routine. On such long days, it is important to maintain a good routine, in order to remain mentally and physically healthy. In fact, even if you do not have particular commitments during the day, it is still important to sleep and wake up early, have breakfast, lunch and dinner at the right times, so as not to upset your biological rhythm too much. If you are not sure how to create a routine, the wikihow.it chapter might be useful.

Cultivate some hobbies. We know that time passes faster when we are busy or when having fun, which is why it is important to cultivate some hobbies, especially as they keep our mind more active. You could therefore take advantage of this surplus of free hours to finally dedicate yourself to something you have always wanted to do, but for various reasons, have always decided to put aside. Remember, doing what you love is the first step to feeling good about yourself.

Meditate. Especially during this time, meditating can help you momentarily forget the situation of distress and danger you are experiencing. It allows you to find an inner balance in all your aspects, bringing harmony to your body, mind and spirit. If you manage to find this balance, you will notice positive effects in your daily life.

Think about the present and set short-term goals. In such a situation, full of fear and indecision about the future, it is easy to feel lost and downcast. Long-term projects and goals appear even more difficult and impossible to achieve, which is why it is important to focus on the present. In addition, setting daily and short-term goals will help you make sense of your days, allowing you to keep your bearings.

LONELINESS

Is loneliness our worst enemy or our best friend?

When you start living alone, one of the first thoughts that comes to mind is the question of loneliness. The moment we think about it, we mistakenly imagine that it is more of a social condition, caused by the absence of people close to us. In fact, it's more of an inner condition. Suffering from loneliness is often the consequence of our continuous flight to the outside. We always try to keep busy with friends, commitments, various activities, but in reality, we do nothing but avoid confrontation with ourselves. Loneliness, therefore, does not necessarily mean being isolated, but mostly represents the space that we share with our inner self and regularly ignore.

Living alone helps you deal with this inner state, because it makes it harder for you to avoid confrontation with yourself. Sooner or later, the period in which you will feel more alone than usual will come, but this should not push you to hole up in a corner to get depressed! On the contrary, I advise you to take the opportunity to dedicate yourself to yourself, both physically and mentally, through the care and discovery of yourself. Once you learn who you really are, it will become easier to love oneself and be alone.

It is also important to know how to disconnect from social media. The latter, even if they allow you to be socially close to the people you love, unconsciously bombard you with the idea of the perfect life. You think other people's lives are great and hassle-free and this leads you to focus more on what you don't have, thus, leading you not to see or appreciate the good things in your life.

Being alone is an advantage because it allows you to focus on your true self, devoid of any social mask. Therefore, loneliness does not necessarily have to be seen as the worst enemy from which one must escape, but as a perfect opportunity to invest in oneself, through self-discovery and self-improvement.

Living alone for many is synonymous with absolute freedom and the absence of rules, but in reality, it is not all that easy. True, there is no one who dictates rules or gives you orders, but you have to face new responsibilities and obligations that were previously taken for granted. It is therefore necessary to learn to take the reins of oneself, establishing one's own rules and limits to avoid totally losing control of one's life. To do this, it is necessary to stop adopting the logic of living alone to have a life of leisure, free of rules and responsibilities. Instead, think of it as the perfect opportunity to show the world that you are mature and responsible enough to be able to get by on your own, especially in difficult times like this.

-

Living alone: 4 main responsibilities to face.

Rental costs and bills to pay. Learn to manage your expenses. Avoid reaching the end of the month with a completely broke current account, especially during this quarantine period. Remember that in reality, because of this situation, you have to be even more careful in managing your purchases. Don't forget that even if you can't go out, there are still many temptations online!

Food shopping to do. Pay attention to the food you buy, not only in monetary terms, but also in quantitative terms. You have to understand that you are alone and that if you overdo it, many things you bought could go bad. Buy the bare essentials without going overboard, especially with easily perishable foods. Remember that even in quarantine, you have to know how to contain yourself! Forced isolation should not be an excuse to rob the supermarket. You will be the only one to eat your groceries and it is certainly not the right time to organize a buffet at home with friends.

House cleaning. Don't adopt the typical logic of: "I'm on my own anyway, I don't care about cleaning." Remember that you too are a person and therefore, deserve to live in a clean place, out of love for you. Plus, it's always nice to be able to welcome any last-minute guests in a clean and tidy environment. During this pandemic period, however, cleaning not only becomes more important, but also represents an excellent pastime.

You are your own doctor. There are no more mom and dad at home, ready to check and heal you. So, avoid the go-go junk foods, which are obviously not good for your health. Remember that if you get sick, there is no one to take care of you, especially during this period!

-

CHAPTER 4: Spend More Time with Your Family and Friends

We assume that being single is not a status that everyone likes!

But thinking that you can never be happy and single at the same time is totally wrong!

Oftentimes, there is a need to have someone by your side, especially when a romantic relationship ends. We close in on ourselves without showing any form of interest and start to feel bad.

Unfortunately, many people are unable to be happy without a partner—a situation that afflicts far too many people and can even lead to more serious problems.

One of these problems is the known emotional addiction that pulls us into toxic relationships. Other problems concern our self-esteem, sometimes so low, that it pushes us to search for someone who loves us for who we are. But, does having a relationship mean being happy?

If we identify what we are really passionate about and we manage, as far as possible, to cultivate it by making our interest an integral part of our life, we will find a happiness that is not necessarily related to a life as a couple.

So, is it possible to be single and happy?

Sure! Being single can bring some unexpected benefits. It is normal to be afraid of being single in a world where love relationships matter so much. Perhaps, the time has come to overcome the fear of being single.

If you think that there is no greater happiness than being in a relationship, you have certainly made the mistake of leaving your happiness in the hands of others; you have allowed your well-being to depend on your relationship with your partner, without considering the fact that you have to be happy for yourself.

"Nobody should have our happiness in their hands."

Try to understand the reasons why you shouldn't be down in the dumps if you find yourself single now. Here are some objective considerations that will make you open your eyes to the possibility of feeling good even alone.

1) We can know ourselves better

Being single, if lived in a functional way, can improve some things about your character, such as the growth of yourself, or even better self-esteem.

Many make the mistake of being convinced that you don't need to be alone to get to know yourself better. Nothing more wrong! Over time, your perception of things and people change. Your experiences inevitably shape your thinking and this leads you to evolve temperamentally. So, take the opportunity to get to know yourself again and rediscover yourself. You will really need it.

2) We can rediscover what we really like

Do you remember when you left the house without having to explain to anyone? When you were not obliged to inform anyone of your movements? Okay, the idea may be tempting, but I prefer not to dwell on these trivial concepts the web is already full of. Being single is not just that! This single condition can bring much more important and tangible benefits, especially from an emotional point of view.

Being single allows you to have more time and space to dedicate to yourself. You can find out what your hobbies, interests and passions are and dedicate yourself to them. You can also expand your network of acquaintances. In this way, you will be able to fortify your identity and even more so, believe in yourself.

3) We can improve ourselves and free ourselves from our past wounds

If the condition of being single is lived well, it helps us to build our personality, work on our defects, strengthen our virtues, and know our qualities as well as our strengths and weaknesses. It also helps us to look at our values and learn from others, to be clear about our desires, what we want and seek, to LOVE ourselves more in order to love someone else.

It helps you to detach yourself from all your hatred, resentments, and bitterness—in short, it helps you heal your wounds. Therefore, before thinking about finding the ideal person, make an effort to be the ideal person yourself.

4) We can be much stronger

When we get used to being with someone and suddenly our situation changes, we feel awkward. We don't know what to do or how our life will go on. Do you know why this happens? Your comfort zone has collapsed and you have been catapulted out of it. Accepting this situation and knowing how to take advantage of it will allow you to be a much stronger person.

5) We can resume relationships with true friends

When we start dating someone, novelty leads us to distance ourselves from our friends, a mistake we easily fall into. Don't you think it's really a pity? Remember: Partners come and go, friends stay. You just have to recover the relationship with those friends, whom you know you can count, even if you have put them aside!

6) We can finally get to know the right person

We cannot be with someone unless we first learn to be alone. If you don't learn to live in that solitude, then your relationship will always be an addiction. You will always try to "fill a void", and this would not help you grow as a couple. It would not allow the birth of an authentic love.

If you want to love, love yourself first, because you can't give something you don't have.

If you want to value, value yourself first, because you won't know the value a person has if you don't first know what you have.

If you want to make someone happy, be happy first, because otherwise, you will only seek your happiness in the other, to the point of making him unhappy.

TO CONCLUDE:

Stop getting frustrated because everyone around you has a partner. In reality, you are not alone. You are with yourself and you are enjoying the time to devote only to you. Life is precious, enjoy the present.

Take your life head on and try to improve it in all possible and imaginable ways. Only in this way will you be able to understand if you are destined to remain alone (as you will feel good about yourself) or destined to meet the person who will be next to you for the rest of your life!

How to make your family understand that you are single but not alone and desperate

You can be single and still be happy and fulfilled. Maybe it's time to figure it out.

At Christmas, at family lunches, at your cousin's or sister's wedding, if you are single, it's never easy to keep the tongues of relatives at bay and these occasions can be a real hassle—especially if you are the only one in this condition and everyone else is coupled.

How many times have you ever heard yourself say "And when do you find a boyfriend?" or, even worse, "do you think you will remain a spinster for life?", arousing different feelings and sensations in you? Even if you want to stay single and dedicate yourself to yourself, there's nothing wrong with that. It isn't written anywhere that a woman has to get engaged and start a family.

Single people are neither lonely nor desperate. Most of them lead full and fulfilling lives. They are surrounded by affection, take care of animals, have fun with friends and play with grandchildren. Still, many feel that it is not possible to be single and happy.

However, if you are not in a relationship, you must not be hurt by the intrusive and indiscreet questions that your relatives may ask you on certain occasions. If you are a single mom or are dealing with a breakup, be prepared to respond with irony and laugh about it. You don't have to be saddened by their comments.

Learn to work on yourself. Think about what's good for you and not care about other people's opinions. Sure, hearing the same phrases over and over can be annoying, but you're happy and that's what matters. How many people are in pairs so as not to be alone? How many feel dissatisfied with their relationship, but are afraid to change? You have chosen freedom, you have chosen to love yourself, to enjoy life, but above all, you have chosen not to waste your time with those who do not deserve you.

So yes, you are single and happy like that.

Keep in touch with your friends when you are single

How to live happily single when all your friends are couples?

Did it happen to you at some point in your life that you were single and look around, seeing only couples among your acquaintances and friends? Unfortunately, this is something that happens very often, especially now that the average age for a marriage is rising.

For a woman, who dreams of a family with children since she was a child, accepting being single can become something very tiring.

Time goes by. Your friends, sisters or younger brothers get married and you go on with your single life. You meet up with others for dinner and feel like an alien when everyone talks about how to organize a wedding or plans to set aside money to buy a house, which of course has one or two more rooms for a child.

We women also have an additional problem: When our friends become mothers, they become monothematic, they only talk about children and often about their diapers. You don't know how someone's gut needs can be topics of conversation, but they care about it to death.

Result: You can't contribute to their conversations and you feel alienated. It doesn't happen to everyone. There are women who deal with the situation in a very relaxed way, without having any problems. They don't think their life is a failure. However, the vast majority of women belong to the first group, even when they don't admit it.

What are the benefits of being single?

I remember vividly, the period of my "singleness" with my own apartment, my own TV, my own bathroom and MIA double walk-in closet.

The bed was also available in its entirety, without anyone invading my half. In the evening, I didn't have to cook; I could decide to eat a sandwich or some leftovers or not eat at all when I return from work. My time was just for me. I could organize my commitments and my fantasies without dividing the minutes among 300 needs.

I could furnish the apartment as I wanted and a woman loves to furnish a house, but, if you have a man close to you who wants to participate, all your personal study on the hottest interior design goes to get fried and every spending on a nice item is considered stupid.

How to deal with single status without feeling bad?

We must learn from the women, the minority, who live single status without a conviction. Fortunately, we live in a society where an unmarried woman can go on living without being on the fringes of society. Of course, after a certain threshold, one may begin to define you as a spinster, but she is a poor idiot and you can go on living without anyone obliging you to marry the first person that comes along or lock yourself up in a convent.

So, learn to deal with your single status without feeling bad by following a few tips.

1- Create alternative relationships

Nowadays, affections are varied and relationships are also possible, so you have alternatives to marriage. Take your eyes off your computer, mobile phone and TV and keep your bonds alive. First of all, spend a lot of time with family and friends. These are relationships that can last a lifetime, in many cases more than a marriage. Do not lose them; feed them all the time.

In a moment of solitude, you can call a friend and it won't be a trivial matter. Offer to babysit children or family pets. You could derive topics for discussion and also feel part of a whole, which for the moment, you cannot yet build by yourself.

2- **Get out of the house more.**

Constantly finds reasons to leave the house and connect with others.

Try new restaurants and shops. If you are a home worker, grab your computer and go to work in a coffee shop. All you need is wi-fi.

Get to know whoever lives near you. In the city, you may tend to have the habit of not knowing who lives next door. For someone like me, who grew up in a country where everyone knows everyone, it's something unusual. If your building is not filled with group of strangers, but of people with whom to chat and have a coffee, you will feel less alone!

3- **Join social groups**

There will be some in your city too. Look for groups dedicated to particular activities and hobbies. These should be people who share a passion with you and therefore, topics of conversation.

4- **Improve your self-esteem**

You have to work on yourself too. Greater social relationships are not a way to overcome the crisis of singleness, if your head does not accept it.

Be proud of yourself. Focus on your career, indulge in new whims like a new dress, tidy hair and so on.

5- **Enjoy private time**

Being alone is not a sentence, you will notice it sooner or later (and you will want to go back). So, enjoy your moments alone. Watch a movie you love, take care of your plants. Explore yourself by writing a journal.

6- **Activate your body**

To overcome loneliness and depression, physical activity is a unique medicine. It is not just about healing the body, but also feeling better about yourself. Running outdoors is the most popular activity. During the summer, you can enjoy a park and it's absolutely free (you don't have the excuse of not having money). If you can't run, you can take long walks.

Choose public paths or popular parks. You could make a lot of friends.

If you have the chance, join the gym. If you are more introverted, finding friends in a closed environment where you always meet the same people will be much easier.

7- Give new life to home

Decor makes us happy, so enjoy. Use bright and warm colors. They will help your mood and build your own private nest.

8- Take your dream trip

Traveling alone is a unique experience that increases our self-esteem and introduces us to ourselves. It is the best way to heal from depression due to single status.

-

I'm the only single in a group of paired friends

In 2016 (the year to which the 2017 study refers), single-person households increased from 20.5% to 31.6%.

Hence, there are many women without partners. Maybe it's you, or you have one in your group of friends. She is that friend, who does not have +1 at parties, who while the other women shake the hand of her partner, squeezes the glass, who watches the couples dance while she is sitting in a corner—a bit like Baby, the protagonist of the *Dirty Dancing* movie. How do you live when you are the only single in a group of friends?

Being the only single should not necessarily lead to sadness. Yet, it happens frequently to feel out of place. This undoubtedly has to do with vulnerability, with our fears, with recurring questions like: "Everyone else has found it, will I ever find love?" Paired friends have their own routine and perhaps the main topics of conversations are cohabitation or children. The only single in the group is there wondering why she is the only one unmatched, when it is not the others who ask. .

On the other hand, it can also happen that you feel the most envied in this group of couples, because you have full use of your freedom and your time. You don't have to consult anyone for your choices, there are no discussions or compromises. The single "entertains" couples with tales of her new acquaintances while they make her feel safe and secure.

What's behind feeling calmer about being the only single in a group of couples?

For some people, dating couples are more painful, while for the author of this story, dating couples allows them to keep negative thoughts at bay. Those who act in this way do so because they find a trick not to directly confront their experiences, with a fragility on which they should reflect. Going out with couples allows you not to expose yourself. It is probably a need that presses from within, that must be elaborated and that must find its own space. By going out with couples, you protect yourself. They represent the canopy capable of sheltering you from a gust of wind.

What does a single person see in other singles?

The idea of going out with another single girl can make us feel in front of the mirror; the other is the bearer of something that is already within us and amplify our sensations. A single woman, dating another single, can see outside of herself, something she identifies with. The image of herself that she sees reflected in the other person can cause a reverberation—a screeching sound. This feeling in the mirror can be difficult. It may feel like a competition. The fact that another girl may be able to win someone in our place can induce a sense of lack. In this case, the competition does not highlight something that the other has more than us, but makes us perceive something that we feel we do not have. Oftentimes, the fiercest judges are right inside us.

What are the differences between dating singles and couples?

When dating couples, it is as if the feeling of being in search of something subsides. When you go out with a single girl, on the other hand, you can see that as aimed at meeting a new partner and having to be "performing." Depending on the people I relate to, a certain type of experience is revived and activated within me and this can cause a certain type of sensation and emotion, a pain for example. At certain periods in life, you feel the need to protect yourself and, consequently, to prefer some types of company over others.

In each of us, there are many needs and fragile aspects. Based on who the other person is and who I am, I may have a tendency to read something about myself in the other person. Seeing other singles as allies, reflected in the positive aspects, is a way out of this impasse.

Some friends represent comfort, others play. It is as if the others were a prism of ourselves. On those mirrors, we find pieces of ourselves. The hope is to integrate all of our wholeness within relationships.

Bear in mind that you can feel very alone even as a couple. In the English language, there are two terms: "Solitude" and "loneliness." The first indicates being alone, understood as a feeling of intimacy towards oneself, a form of pleasure in being with oneself, a state of self-nourishment and fulfillment, while the second indicates a state of isolation, lack and suffering.

Should one engage more in self-nurturing to find happiness?

Self-feeding means learning to take care of yourself, to feel complete. When we go to the cinema or to the museum alone, people wonder why. They are amazed and probably think it's sad. They use units of measurement in relation to existence. But, one is not half of two. It is simply different from two. It is not hierarchically below. When I go to the cinema alone, I am self-nourished—same as when I go to the sea, to an exhibition, or take a walk. Taking care of yourself is like being your own mother / father / friend / girlfriend. We should also understand what is behind the "need" to be with someone else, what it means for us to have a relationship. Let's not forget that serenity is an individual condition. There are those who are unhappy alone and those who are unhappy being in a relationship. Being single is not the same as being sad or frustrated.

-

CHAPTER 5: Comfort Zone - The Beginning of Your Life

Comfort zone: What it is, how to get out of it and what you need to know to really start your life.

The experiences that matter are often the ones we never wanted to do, not the ones we decide to do. For years, we have heard about this comfort zone, but what is it? The comfort zone is not a new concept, but it is always effective to understand what it is to be able to change your life. In this chapter, you will understand what exactly the comfort zone is, why it is so important to get out of it from time to time and how to leave it with a reasonable dose of safety.

What is the comfort zone?

The comfort zone is your own psychological area where everything is familiar, that sphere where you have no difficulty in moving freely and in which you always feel at ease, free from stress and anxiety. If you try to think about it, you experience it every day, when you choose a familiar place rather than a new one, or when you talk to your usual friends, instead of making new acquaintances. This type of attitude is manifested for protection. If you feel insecure, your brain will try to protect you from any dangers. Generally, staying in your comfort zone is as pleasant as lounging under the covers.

Let me be clear, there is nothing wrong with this, but by systematically following this attitude, you will always find yourself moving around in your little handkerchief of emotions without ever trying something really new.

Why should we bother venturing outside the comfort zone? At this point, you will already have realized that if you don't get out of your mental limits, you will never grow up and your comfort zone will become your prison. If you have a hard time imagining yourself doing something uncomfortable, try to think of all the good things you've got in life, whether small or big ones. You will realize that you have got the best results out of your area of comfort. Many times you have gotten a benefit, you came out of your comfort zone, perhaps, without realizing it. Maybe, when you have finally joined the gym, or when you have asked for that person's number, try to think about it carefully.

Comfort zone

Experience is acquired by leaving the comfort zone, and gradually putting yourself in situations, in which you do not feel completely comfortable. If you do not start to leave this enclosure, you will never improve your livability area.

Challenges are fun. Getting out of the comfort zone must not only be an inconvenience, but also a little fun— daring is half living, as the saying goes. Now that you have realized this truth, start reflecting on those moments when you have taken these small steps, and think positively about it. The personal success you are looking for is not in the comfort zone, otherwise, you would have already achieved it without difficulty. It is outside and to take it, you have to enter your learning zone.

By expanding your comfort zone, you will go to a thin anti-panic zone, which will gradually transform into a teaching area.

I guess now you understand that you have experienced the comfort zone many times and that getting out of it in a controlled way is essential to achieve your success.

Signs that we are stuck in the comfort zone:

Now let's see what alarm bells indicate that we have been stuck in the comfort zone for too long.

We have not been growing for a long time, both professionally and personally.

Our relationships do not evolve and do not mature. We no longer feel that pleasant rush of energy that goes through us when we want to dedicate ourselves to a new project.

We haven't been learning anything new in a long time. We have always followed the same routines and habits and the days fly by without us realizing it. We see the risk of making mistakes as something to be avoided at all costs.

We don't feel much different than we did ten or more years ago. These may just be a few signs, but if you recognize yourself in them, you are probably stuck in your comfort zone.

So, let's see how to get out of these limiting stakes. Getting out of your sphere of control is not easy. To do it effectively you need to take small steps.

The idea therefore is to push yourself into the learning zone, avoiding the panic zone.

To do this, you can help yourself with these 4 tricks.

 # 1. A pinch of madness

Without throwing yourself headlong into real madness, try to take life as it happens. Don't care what other people think; you will be criticized anyway. If you don't stick your nose out of your comfort zone because you fear the judgment of others, you are wasting time. You will always be criticized by someone.

Live your life by seizing even the most particular occasions. It may turn out bad—or not. The important thing is not to remain confined to your usual routine of controlled and predictable events.

2. Act in company

Getting out of the comfort zone can be difficult. To simplify the task a little, at the beginning, you can get help from a person close to you. Divide the stressful load. You can deal with these situations alone, having experience in your discomfort. This system is perhaps the most effective for entering the learning zone in a controlled manner.

3. Change your perspective

The unknown is not always to be feared. Sometimes, it can turn into a powerful spring to accomplish extraordinary things. In the past, most brilliant people have challenged the unknown, understanding how this could give them the impetus to get involved, addressing the unknown as something to be known and explored—not to be feared. Appreciating what you do not know will encourage you to look around and no longer settle for your comfort zone.

4. Accept the discomfort

Accepting the fact that getting out of the comfort zone will lead to anxiety and stress is the first step to take. We must understand that to grow, to improve and to change our life, it is necessary to gradually expose ourselves to discomfort.

Life begins outside the comfort zone as you will have understood. The secret to getting out of your comfort zone is to get involved and do it in small doses. A minimum risk is essential to act. The important thing is that it is an acceptable risk, thoughtful and manageable.

Making friends with this type of unknown is essential to avoid living confined to your mental cage. The ideal strategy is to do something you like but are a little afraid of, so as to make the experience fun and rewarding.

-

CHAPTER 6: Enjoy Your Freedom

The issue of loneliness and isolation is a "hot" and very topical issue. We live on a planet where people are mostly annoyed with one another, if not hostile.

The majority suffer from loneliness even in a crowd, in the family, or as a couple.

There are people who feel alone despite having a husband or wife and children, even in families where the level of conflict is not high.

On the other hand, there are people who find it impossible to be happy alone. You don't have to resign to being alone.

The point is, it is useful to reach the awareness that by truly learning to feel good in an autonomous and independent way, we open ourselves to others and open ourselves to the possibility—and the concrete opportunity—to be happy with others, rather than being with others while still feeling lonely and unhappy.

Being with others, particularly in pairs, and feeling lonely, is typical of dysfunctional and dependent relationships, so it's really helpful to find out how to be happy alone, in order to be happy with others.

When you are in love, you believe that the love you feel has a lucky outcome, you feel on top of the world. There is no person who, when in love, has not experienced feelings of almost omnipotence: Euphoria, greater ability to concentrate, higher self-esteem, and very high confidence in oneself and ones surroundings. It is no surprise that many people who have not been in a relationship for a long time suddenly realize that many are looking for them and find them fascinating, when they finally find a partner

Numerous scientific studies have been done on this subject, by authoritative researchers, and it has been shown that the feeling of being a superhero or a superheroine given by falling in love is due to the greater production, by some areas of the brain, of certain neurotransmitters and hormones—the main one being dopamine.

Dopamine regulates the mechanism of desire and reward. For example, its production rises after having had a satisfactory sexual intercourse, after a desired result has been achieved, after having received a gratification. It may also be activated in dysfunctional ways, through addictions, such as consumption of cocaine.

So, if you want to increase dopamine production, you can take cocaine, become addicted to something—like gambling, slot machines, an unknown person that you fell in love with via chat, that may sooner or later try to extort money from you and you think it's for love, a destructive relationship with a bastard who plays the cycle of abuse with you.

I admit and recognize that the "magical" combination of patterns, exchanges and sensations that occur when one is in love is unlikely to repeat itself in other situations, even if there are many human, functional experiences that come close to something similar.

At the same time, it is really worth discovering how to be happy alone, using the mechanisms of our physiology and biochemistry to our advantage. Dopamine, neurotransmitters and hormones aside, certain activities and a certain mental attitude are good in themselves.

How do we fall in love with ourselves, produce more dopamine and other hormones of happiness and enthusiasm, and become more likeable, not only to others, but also to ourselves?

I offer you 25 (twenty-five!) Practical tips to be happy alone

"From time to time, it is good to take a break in our pursuit of happiness and simply be happy."

Guillame Apollinaire

Take care of yourself. This means everything and it means nothing. In fact, I aim to take care of myself in a "holistic" way, from a physical and emotional point of view. Keep reading.

Give yourself a "regulation", that is, follow the daily rules that help establish a positive routine and habits: Make your bed, have regular meals at fixed times, get up and go to bed at the same time. Set up a ritual for the self-care, for meals, for the time of going to sleep, gauge and balance the hours of rest, work and leisure.

Get regular health checks based on your age and personal needs. Follow the therapies prescribed by accredited doctors, whose competence is known and trusted.

Exercise. Doing physical activity, appropriate to your level of training, your health and your wellness needs, is never wrong. Exercising allows you to produce a whole range of substances that are good for you, to sweat and eliminate toxins and to release stress and nervousness.

Take care of your living and working environment. Clean up (without getting obsessed) and make the places where you live more welcoming. This communicates a message to yourself: "I deserve the best and I know how to create it for myself."

Eat properly and drink fluids in the right amount.

Take care of your *personal hygiene* and your appearance. For the same reasons as in point three.

Shop carefully and dedicate yourself to cooking or learning to cook well, not only in a healthy way, but also tasty, as well as on a regular basis, especially if you have lunch or dinner alone.

Take care of your finances, that is, your money. Decide to learn how to manage them effectively.

Read books of various genres, to broaden your horizons and learn about the points of view and experiences of others. It also helps you to realize that many suffer or have suffered for various reasons, not necessarily loneliness. You may also find that man have managed to achieve well-being in the midst of grief and suffering.

Be in contact with nature from time to time, if you are used to being in the chaos of the city or. Conversely, go into the frenzy of the city from time to time, if you are used to being with nature.

Vary the activities in your day and in your existence.

Watch comedy movies and videos for a good laugh.

Get used to *laughing at yourself*, rather than getting angry or mistreating yourself.

Behave in a frivolous, childish and playful way when you feel like it. This includes hopping, humming, singing, singing in "gramelot" (i.e. in an invented language) as we did as children. Sing with your mouth closed. Grimace in front of the mirror. Imitate famous people and much more.

Sleep and rest when tired.

When you want to become carnally united with your sofa because you are taken by sadness and melancholy, make an act of will and move. Stand up, do some small housework, or take a shower. Brush your teeth and / or face, hair, or go out for a walk. Dance at home, in the park or in the garden.

Turn off that damn smartphone, mobile, tablet, laptop, or any other tool that lets you enter the web or social media, particularly Facebook or WhatsApp. Turn it off and forget it for at least a couple of hours a day. In general, minimize its usage as much as possible.

Instead of pouring anger, depression and complaints on social media, keep a diary to write them down. Write those things that have created small or large frustrations daily or over a period of time. We make our lives worse just because of a misunderstanding with a stranger on the bus, the delay of a colleague at work or for having lost a glove of little value, simply because we needed or were fond of it. The awareness of our frailties is useful to overcome them.

Meditation serves to increase dopamine production. It happens that those who are already overloaded with obligations embark on learning disciplines that are not always so useful in our world. This includes meditation. Meditation means emptying the mind and focusing it on the present moment. You can meditate quietly by washing the dishes, tidying up the house, drying clothes, taking a walk, cycling (not in traffic), lying on your back, with your legs against the wall and looking at your feet, and relaxing on the sofa.

Having sex for sex, without obligation. It is allowed, did you know? You can have sex with someone who is good to have sex with, without having to fall in love with them and/ or be forced to suffer.

Thinking and reflecting on the past. **Oh my God, hasn't the past passed?** Yes, of course, a sad and troubled past must be forgotten and left behind in the past. Instead, it may be useful to research the past of one's family, community or country: What were the lifestyles of our parents when they were little? What about our grandparents? What about our great-grandparents? What did they eat? How did they dress? How did they spend their free time? These "time travels" to discover something that basically belongs to us and is part of us, even if we do not know it, allows us to expand our existential dimension and make us richer.

Learn to *distinguish good from evil,* even in small things. Get used to changing your mind, when necessary. We often get caught up in prejudices about episodes and people and we tend to always see negatives. In reality, it is more useful to listen and observe on a case-by-case basis and decide from time to time what is negative or positive.

Give yourself to others. This does not mean starting to be a Red Cross nurse as if there were no tomorrow. It means dedicating oneself to a few people who deserve our attention, offering availability and generosity without a grant, but according to the possibilities we have—without taking anything away from our life.

-

CHAPTER 7: Starting A New Hobby by Being Single

Everyone needs to carve out a few moments of relaxation between the constant commitments of the week. It is not just about being able to find time to go to the beautician or having coffee with friends. It is necessary to find something more stable and continuous. A hobby, for example. We often forget how important it is to do something that helps to disconnect with the mind and feel better about yourself, and therefore with others. Here are some ideas to put into practice, alone or with friends.

Playing sports

Exercising is ideal for combining the useful and enjoyable. The proposals, however, are endless. How then? Just choose from those that best match your lifestyle and schedule. You can go for a run in the morning and feel energetic for the rest of the day. You can do yoga to become more aware of your body. There are also many new forms of exercise to release tension and stay fit. Among the stars, for example, cross fit is crazy: A very hard work out that combines free body, cardio activity and weights. If you are a water lover, you can have the option of a swimming or water aerobics course. The important thing is to start.

Another very popular opportunity for recreation among the outbreaks is the attendance of sports clubs, chosen above all by those looking for a great way to unwind after work and the opportunity to meet new friends and possible partners. Teamwork and collaboration can give an unexpected twist to the day.

Gardening

Growing flowers and plants may seem like a simple thing, but it isn't. It takes patience, dedication and a handful of knowledge. Those who practice gardening, however, are ready to praise its immense talents and studies seem to prove them right. In fact, it has been shown that taking care of a small garden or even just balcony plants helps to significantly reduce stress and improve mood. There are many books that help you get started with small and simple tips. If that isn't enough, many nurseries organize special courses for anyone who decides to develop a green thumb.

Sign up for a dance class

You do not need to have music in your blood to be able to dance. Beyond the disciplines that you learn as a child, such as ballet, there are many dance classes for adults to do alone, as a couple or with friends. Latin Americans have been dictating the law for some time, but in recent years, sensual dances such as tango or those linked to popular traditions, such as the Apulian pizzica have also taken hold. All it takes is a little courage and self-irony.

Dance courses represent an excellent opportunity to combine healthy movement with the possibility of making new acquaintances. Group dances, particularly popular with single girls, are one of the most immediate ways to meet a large number of new people, who may later become friends or dating companions.

Dedicate yourself to DIY

If you love to take care of your home and make something with your own hands, DIY is for you. No special skills are needed, just a few books or tutorials on the internet to get ideas to actualize. Thanks to the proliferation of vintage markets, it is possible to find objects that need small adjustments. Start here and allow yourself be carried away by creativity.

Learning a foreign language

Languages are increasingly important nowadays. Knowing English is often a discriminating factor when looking for a job. However, it is now essential for anyone who loves to travel and learn about the world, to learn other languages. The courses to learn languages are endless, both traditional and online. If you want to save money and learn to speak quickly, look for a foreign native speaker to chat with at the bar, over coffee or via Skype, offering to teach him Italian. This is an au pair exchange that can be useful as well as fun.

Learn to (get) massages

Who doesn't like massages? Instead of just spending an hour relaxing every now and then, you can try learning how to do them. There are many schools that offer courses for beginners. You could spend a few hours a week with friends and put what you have learned into practice on them, making the money spent on the course pay off. If you are too lazy, you can always treat yourself to the afternoon at the spa.

Learn cutting and sewing

New fashion or return to traditions? Knitting and learning to sew are activities that in recent years, have attracted millions of followers, even among younger women. You don't need to have big skills; you start small with the simplest techniques and then move on. There are a lot of courses for this in Italy. Go to YouTube and discover that there is a real community of wire addicts. What are you waiting for to be part of it?

The art of photography

If you are a person attentive to detail, with a particular eye for nature and its wonders, photography can give you emotions. Just go out into the fresh air and be inspired by what the world has to offer. The only downside is the cost of good equipment. Camera prices aren't exactly low, but you can start with the simpler, cheaper models, before making a bigger investment.

Making candles

Candles help to warm up a room and make it more comfortable. What you may not know is that candles are easy to make at home too. On the net, there are many tips that will enable you make them on your own, without difficulty. This saves money and prevents the wastage of remains of those already burned.

Sign up for a cooking class

For many people, the kitchen is a place to relax and unwind. Inventing new recipes and learning how to make them can be very satisfying. Even if you are an expert cook, you can always sign up for a specific cooking class to learn some particular techniques. The popular techniques at the moment are the cake design courses that teach how to create colorful and decorated cakes, like those you see on television.

Speed holidays

Traveling is one of the watchwords of singles, who are not afraid to go on an adventure and discover new places, even alone, aware of being able to make new friends during their stay. Exotic destinations with crystalline and dreamy seas, cruise holidays, thematic weekends, are just some possible types of holidays for singles to enjoy the brackets of relaxation and fun.

THE FOOD

The passion of the breakout for food and cooking is well known, but it has grown so much in recent times that there are more and more singles who, among the various courses they enroll, choose the cooking and pastry courses that are so fashionable in recent times. Knowing how to prepare delicious and original dishes is always a good ace in the hole. On a romantic date, you may arrive halfway down the path of seduction with an excellent dinner!

A BOOK

Reading a good book is certainly one of the most transversal hobbies, but many challengers love to carve out moments of their free time to devote to the great classics of literature and the most exciting news coming out in the bookstore. Do not underestimate the collections of poems for the most romantic singles.

COLLECTING

Model making and collecting are also very popular pastimes—one of the first hobbies to make their way through the activities to be dedicated to free time. Planes, cars and motorcycles to be assembled are the privileged object of this practice. Above all, collecting (such as coasters and caps, vintage objects, action figures from films or series) is a hobby that always carves out an important place, alongside other more dynamic pastimes.

7 CREATIVE HOBBIES TO START AT HOME

1) VLOGGING

From your personal experiences to your dreams, YouTube is the ideal platform to tell what is happening around you.

After all, this Covid-19 is the best time to launch your own YouTube channel.

Choose a theme you are passionate about—like travel or fashion. Create some conversational topics, set up the camera and play. Let's start with the recording. For the first time, you can always shoot with an iPhone. If you like it and want to go to the next level, you can buy a professional camera, as I suggest in this chapter.

A) INTRODUCTION TO THE CHANNEL

If you are about to activate a channel, then don't forget to shoot an introductory video. Tell your potential viewers something extraordinary, who you are, what you do and what you hope to achieve through your channel.

To most people, you're still a stranger, so they need to get to know you better before they know if they want to subscribe to your vlog and start following you.

B) WHY ARE YOU VLOGGING

If there is a reason you want to become a professional vlogger, then your first video will be a great way to explain why. Maybe you're hoping to start making some pennies (it's always very low) or it's just a nice way to grab attention and share your experiences with people.

C) FUTURE PROJECTS

Tell your potential viewers what they will see on your channel in the future, what kind of videos you will make, how often you will upload and what topics you will cover.

D) TELL YOUR PERSONAL BATTLES

We all have our own personal battles. Opening a discussion on this type of topic is a great way to create a special feeling with your audience, as it shows that you are human.

2) CREATE A PODCASTING

In the age of social distancing and personal isolation, many of us crave conversation and interaction with others.

That's where Podcasting comes in.

Podcasts are a great excuse to be able to talk to other people living in other countries. You can start podcasting with something as simple as an app, then move on to a more professional platform.

A) PLANNING

This is the often-overlooked initial stage of creating a winning podcast. I highly recommend that you spend a lot of time on this first point before moving on.

Feel free to go out with a notebook or whiteboard. These will help you to write down all the ideas that come to you during the day.

Talk to your family, ask your friends, compare yourself with people who may have already tried, firsthand, what it means to open a Podcast.

B) CHOOSE A TOPIC

Do you want your Podcast to be focused on a particular topic or would you rather have a little bit of everything talked about?

If you decide to deal with a specific niche, I assure you that you will be much more successful.

Try to narrow down on something that you can talk about for many episodes (over a hundred) but not so narrow that it cannot attract a good chunk of the audience.

C) CHOOSE A NAME

Choosing the right name for your podcast can be really tricky. You want the title to perfectly describe what your show is about, but you also want to entertain and attract people who casually pass through your channel.

After all, when a user goes through your podcast, they should immediately understand what topic you are talking about. I always see too many podcasters who, in order to appear nice, choose a name that is a little too out of the ordinary, but which basically only serves to confuse viewers.

D) CHOOSE A CO-CONDUCTOR

Do you have a friend, business partner or colleague you prefer to start with?

Starting a podcast with someone can be a lot easier. You will surely have a more engaging conversation if you both decide to share your views on a specific topic.

Plus, you can split your other podcasting related activities like marketing, promotion and more.

E) CREATE A LOGO FOR YOUR PODCAST

Once the podcast is planned, it's time to choose a logo. The logo, in fact, will be your brand, which is why it is essential that you take all the time you need to come up with a creative concept.

Creating a good logo has several advantages:

- The logo is the key element that defines your digital identity.
- The logo increases your brand awareness, improves the image of your website and makes your podcast more popular in its target audience, thus increasing user loyalty.
- A logo ensures that your content is authentic and protects it from counterfeiting.

A) CANVA

Canva is a completely free app that will help you create a great logo.

Once you have created your account and logged in, click on *Create a project > Logo* and start playing with the different options that the site offers.

You can also choose one of the many predefined templates, customize it with the name of your podcast.

B) FIVERR

If you don't feel like you can make a logo yourself, I suggest you go to Fiverr.

Fiverr is an online marketplace made by freelancers for freelancers. Just create an account, and after logging in, you can choose your logo from the hundreds of offers that the site offers you.

C) FREELOGODESIGN

Free Logo Design is a free logo maker for entrepreneurs, small businesses, freelancers and associations to create professional-looking logos in minutes.

D) RENDERFOREST

Renderforest is a video creation platform that allows small businesses and bloggers to easily create explanatory videos with the aim of increasing and converting their users.

The peculiarity of this platform is that it is based on Cloud Storage, so it will not be necessary to install any type of software to use it.

Of course, in addition to creating videos, Renderforest also creates fantastic logos to use for their platforms.

3) BEGIN WITH THE PHOTO EDITING

I know, in the last few years you have taken so many pictures, but you have abandoned them there, in the hard disk you bought last week. True?

Well, it's time to go inside your archive, choose the photos you like best and start working on them with the fantastic Adobe Creative Cloud programs.

Editing photos will not only help you develop your creativity, but will also be able to curb your craving for travel (which Covid-19 prevents you from doing), giving you the opportunity to remember and treasure the wonderful moments you have created.

4) DANCE

If you're looking for an activity that mixes creativity with exercise, then why not consider dancing? On the web, you will find dozens and dozens of online resources that will help you learn the new steps of some semi-unknown dance.

After all, the health benefits of dance are amazing. In addition to physical training, with the dance, you will stimulate the learning areas of the brain, which have been shown to make you healthier and more active.

There are hundreds of different dance styles, so the first thing to do is to choose the style you would like to focus on.

Personally, I am a fan of these types of dance:

- Hip Hop
- Funky
- Street Dance
- Breakdance
- Belly dance
- Samba
- Cha cha cha
- Merengue
- Bachata
- Tap Dance
- Waltz

Choose your style, open YouTube and type *course*, followed by the name of the dance you have chosen.

5) LEARN TO MAKE VIDEOS

In my opinion, filmmaking is one of the most fascinating and most fulfilling professions in the world. Having all day to deal with lights, actors, sets and so on, will give you a charge that few professions in the world can give.

If you want to start working with video making, then don't waste any more time. Pick up your iPhone and start shooting videos of your family, your dog, your building, what you see from the window of your room, in short, shoot everything that comes to mind and then, as soon as you can, check the shot on the PC.

This way you will notice which the most serious mistakes are, where you could improve or maybe what you could buy to make that particular movement, slightly more fluid.

6) OPEN A BLOG AND START WRITING

Starting a blog and starting to write could become a cure for the soul for many people.

The problem is, they don't know.

Yes, in addition to having fun, I also make money.

Obviously, before starting to make money with a blog, you will have to study web marketing in depth, and put everything you have learned into practice.

I admit, it wasn't easy, but with the strength of perseverance, you have the ability to truly get anywhere. Speaking of perseverance, recently, I saw the film "The Founder" for the first time. It tells the story of the founder of one of the most famous restaurants in the world: "McDonald's."

In the very first minutes of the film, a voiceover reads:

"Perseverance!

Nothing in the world can replace perseverance.

Neither talent... what is more common than talented men who are not successful?

Neither genius...unrewarded genius is in fact commonplace.

Neither is education. The world is full of educated fools.

Only perseverance and determination are omnipotent.

Prove that nothing can ever defeat you. That you can achieve serenity, better health and a never-ending flow of energy.

If you set yourself the achievement of these goals every single day, the results will not take long to manifest themselves clearly.

While it may seem like a magic formula to you, it is within you that you build your future.

The greatest discovery of my generation is that human beings can change their life by changing their mental attitude.

Or, as Ralph Emerson argued, a man is what he thinks, all day long! "

7) WRITE POEMS

Writing poetry doesn't require any kind of accessories and is a great way to develop ingenuity and creativity at the same time. So, don't delay. Grab a pen and paper right away and start jotting down some initial topics. It could be something personal or maybe something that is happening right now in the world.

Once your ideas are clear, focus and start writing.

A) READ MANY POEMS

If you want to write poetry, start reading other people's poems.

You can do it randomly, by typing some poet's name you find on the web, or you can start by analyzing the phrases of poems that have struck you most.

B) FOCUSED ON THE OBJECTIVE

Before you start writing a poem, ask yourself where you would like to go with it. Would you like to explore a personal experience of yours, for example, a social injustice? Or do you prefer to talk about the sky, the clouds or your cat?

The choice is yours.

Once you understand the topic, start writing with your goal in mind.

And never forget it!

C) AVOID SENTIMENTALISM

Please, stop with these poems that speak only of love.

Susan Minot, the great American screenwriter (the one who wrote "I dance alone", so to speak), says that too much sentimentality can destroy any type of literary work. If your poem is too sappy, your readers may rebel because they understand that you want to affect them emotionally.

Writing about feelings is a gift that God has granted to a few.

D) DON'T OBSESS ON THE FIRST WORDS

If you feel that you haven't been able to spell the first few words correctly, don't give up.

Keep writing and go back to the very first words when you are more ready. The first line is just one component of a much more complex work of art.

8) KITCHEN

If you want to start cooking, know that the internet is full of sites and videos that only talk about cooking.

-

CHAPTER 8: Types of Single Men and Why They Like to Live Alone

-

The fact is that, those who decide to live alone by choice or not, are constantly increasing. Do not think that bachelors are all the same. There are different types, some very common, others rarer, which together make up the diverse universe of singles.

The mammon

The forty-year-old who lives at home with his parents is a classic. Someone had called him big baby but in reality, he is a very nice sly. He is served and revered by his mother whom he venerates as an ancient Greco-Roman deity. She always has lunch and dinner with her favorite dishes, fragrant clothes, well-ironed shirts and her own room with full control of the TV remote. Should he leave this paradise in the name of love or independence? What they say, a true single by choice!

The convinced

Here you need seriousness because you don't mess around with a convinced single. Living alone is a real mission. He goes straight on his way without looking anyone in the face. Not even the piles of dirty laundry scattered around the house and the piles of dishes to wash in the kitchen disturb him. It is the minimum price to pay in the name of freedom. Do you want to recognize one? The next time you go to the supermarket, pay attention to that man in his thirties who, with his yellow basket, is intent on shopping. It's easy to spot because he wanders between the canned food aisle and the frozen food aisle. There is no fresh food in his purchases. The watchword is long shelf life and his ideal dinner is tuna in oil, which he does not even remove from the box, to save a dish to wash.

The disappointed

The disappointed single is a young man with a hopelessly broken heart. What he believed to be the love of his life has left him like a dog on the ring road. He has decided that he will never experience such pain again and that the best solution is to live alone. As we know, between saying and doing, there is the sea, and experience teaches us that it is an absolutely temporary condition. He was not born to be single; he cannot be alone even for 5 minutes. It may not be today and maybe not even tomorrow, but sooner or later, he will end up again in the soft embrace of love.

The unfortunate

There is little to do here. When Mother Nature gets up on the wrong foot and decides to stick with it, you have to give up. How is it said? Appearance doesn't matter and the important thing is to be beautiful inside! In real life, things are quite different. To you, who are a cross between the unwatchable and the obscene, I grant the honor of arms and the possibility of shouting with pride and pride that you are single by choice. Even if the choice is not theirs, we are not to nitpick. A little understanding is required for those who have suffered the wrath of Mother Nature.

The survivor

He is a warrior, who after his third marriage, went up in smoke and had three substantial maintenance checks to be paid every month, has wisely decided to join the army of singles. Better late than never! After being tested by many battles and survived the war, he can finally enjoy his newfound freedom, watching the game in religious silence and sleeping in the double bed diagonally.

The genetically driven

This is the rarest type. It is the single who has the loneliness gene. If being with a woman for just one week counts as a romantic relationship, then even this type of single can say they have had a romantic relationship. You could call it misanthropic or asocial, but you'd be wrong. He is simply mentally predisposed to be single. His life is organized down to the smallest detail. He loves having everything under control and he is a freak of order. There is no shortage of opportunities to decide to change his life, but he has no idea of doing it. He organizes his trips alone or with a few friends; he lives in true and absolute freedom. You will wonder if this doesn't bore him. Obviously not, after all, he has genetics on his side. He is the one and only true single by choice.

CHAPTER 9: Appreciate Life

Everyone has experienced this feeling at least once. You know you have everything you should be grateful for in life: An important person by your side, a loving family, a good job, a healthy, functioning body. Nonetheless, you feel this overwhelming feeling of frustration, as if what you have is not enough. Sure, you might be happier by making some changes in your life, but the easiest way to feel better and appreciate what you have is to change your perspective and routine. So, how do you start enjoying the sun instead of complaining about sunburn? By following these steps.

Part 1: Changing Perspective

1. Live in the present. The happiest people are those who are able to enjoy their present rather than remain anchored in the past or become obsessed with what the future holds for them. It is true that reflecting on the past can help us learn from our mistakes and focus on the future can help us plan goals and make long-term projects, yet to be happy with what we have, we must also know how to appreciate the now. Focus on what this day is giving you, rather than thinking about what happened yesterday or how much you might change tomorrow.

Close your eyes and take a few deep breaths. Focus on the precise moment you are living and all your worries will disappear. Be patient, this exercise takes some practice.

You can also meditate or do yoga to help you stay focused on the present rather than worrying about the future.

2. **Be grateful for what you have.** Instead of focusing on everything you miss or want, take a minute to think about how lucky you are compared to the majority of people out there. While your life may not be perfect, there are certainly some things you can feel truly grateful for, be it your wonderful family, your wonderful friends, the beautiful romance you are having, your health, your job, the beautiful city where you live or your beloved home. Chances are, you don't have all of these things (hardly does anyone have them all), but surely, some of them are a part of your life and are enough to be thankful every day.

Write a list of things to be thankful for every Sunday, to remind yourself of all the good things in your life.

Take the time to thank the people who help you; you can do it in person or write a letter.

Spend more time surrounded by nature. This will make you feel even more grateful, reminding you how much beauty surrounds you.

3. **Appreciate the little things.** Feel grateful for the air you breathe, the food you eat, the quiet of your home—

every little detail counts in life. Focus on these little things and think about the luck of being alive. Reflect on the love your dog has for you, on the bakery down the street where you usually have a great breakfast, the beautiful climate of your region or your beautiful library full of books. There is no need to think of something stellar, just focus on small things that will help you realize how much happiness that surround you.

Even if you've had a terrible day, try to think of three little things that made it worth living. Maybe an unexpected email has come in from an old friend, you had a nice conversation with your neighbor, or had a great coffee for breakfast.

4. Take the time to reflect. Many people are not happy with their life because they don't stop to consider everything that happens around them. You can do this by writing a diary at the end of the day or once a week; maybe take long walks to relax or just sit in the middle of nature to think about what happened to you during the day. This doesn't mean getting down on yourself, overthinking, or focusing on all the things that went wrong. However, take the time to rationally evaluate everything that happens in your life.

Getting used to reflection is useful for thinking rationally when a problem arises, thus, preventing tough times from catching us off guard.

5. Don't compare yourself to anyone. It's another way to be unhappy. Don't think about how big your neighbor's house is, your friend's good job, and don't compare your troubled relationship with your best friend's perfect one. You cannot change what happens to others and you will not go anywhere by comparing yourself with them. Focus on your life. .

You will always find someone happier, healthier, richer and more beautiful than you. But, why should you care?

You may be very envious of your friend's relationship, but he may envy your wonderful career. There is always something to be jealous of, but others also find reasons to envy you. If you completely stop comparing yourself to the people around you, you will be doing yourself a nice favor.

If you go to Facebook just to find out who's engaged, who's got a new job, who's gone on vacation, and so on, it's time to stop. Because of social media, you will get the feeling that whatever you have will never be enough.

6. Pretend until you're convinced it's true. Even if you're feeling down, don't walk around downcast, complaining, telling all your friends how bad you feel and with the expression of someone about to cry. Instead, you should try to be even more brilliant, very friendly, making an effort to talk to people and make them smile. It doesn't mean that you have to hide the deepest sadness and pain, but if you are feeling a little down for no serious reason, you should put an extra effort into looking happy. You will be surprised to find out how quickly this "fiction" will fool your mind and make you feel happier!

Sure, sharing your problems with a friend can help you solve them. But, getting angry and complaining to everyone who hears you, will only make you feel worse.

7. Take the time to listen to your sadness. Dr. David Spiegel, director of the Center for Integrative Medicine at

Stanford University, reminds us that, "Happiness is not the absence of sadness." This means that you can be happy even when dealing with negative emotions and allowing yourself to cry. Pretending to be spirited when you are experiencing something really serious doesn't make you happier.

Some suffering will make you appreciate the best things in your life, making you even more grateful for what you have.

By talking to friends about your sadness, you will have the feeling that you have more control over your life, which will make you happier.

8. Know that money doesn't change things as much as you think. Certainly, having more money will change appearances, but the fundamentals will remain the same. You might be driving a fancy car, owning nicer clothes, having a bigger house with three guest rooms. In the long run, you won't be happy anymore. If you have enough money to pay for basic necessities and have some fun, more income will not have an exorbitant effect on your happiness.

Sure, revamping your wardrobe would make you feel better in the short term, but over time, you will remain the same person—only dressed better.

9. Have genuine compassion for others. Tenzin Gyatso, the fourteenth Dalai Lama, said, "If you want others to be happy, practice compassion; if you want to be happy, practice compassion." Part of happiness lies in making connections with others and recognizing the suffering of others. Building compassion for others will help you build stronger relationships, not obsess over yourself and feel less alone in the world. The next time you are with someone else, consider things from their point of view, rather than worrying about what you look like. You will feel happier immediately.

It takes practice to develop compassion. The more time you spend with people, the faster you will acquire this form of empathy.

10. Remember that happiness is a choice. Some people measure it by considering their career, car, or bank savings. Happiness, however, cannot be determined by anything material. It is a choice; we can be happy regardless of what life offers us. Start working on it by telling yourself "I'm happy to be who I am."

Being happier today, according to a study, is also an indicator of the contentment you will experience in the future. So, choosing to be happy has effects that go beyond the present.

Several studies also reveal that happier people have fewer health problems. This decision therefore also affects physical well-being.

-

Part 2: Change your Actions

1. Don't let the sun go down on anger. Some people think that if something makes you angry, you should say it right away to prevent the feeling of rage from escalating. Of course, in some cases, this is true. Some other times, anger is a passing feeling that disappears by going to bed and forgetting what has bothered us. The next time something not very serious is bothering you, ask yourself, "Does this really deserve to be highlighted?" or "Will I care that much when I have a different mood?" If the answer is no, don't dwell on this emotion.

Certainly, there are those who think that you should never go to bed angry. Others, on the other hand, believe that if you stop giving importance and talking about everything that bothers you, you get less angry.

2. Simplify your life. People who rejoice in their lives typically don't have many things to worry about. They only have what they need, they don't have a wardrobe full of clothes. They have a car in the family, rather than two or three, so they don't have to worry too much about maintenance costs. They have a credit card instead of three, four close friends instead of fifty acquaintances, and they focus on the few things they love, instead of engaging in a lot of things they are only marginally interested in.

Look around. Do you really need so many pairs of shoes? Two types of iPods? Three calendars hanging on the desk? Whenever you can delete something, do it.

Tidying up is another way to make life easier. Clean all surfaces and drawers, both at work and at home, eliminating everything you don't need. You will feel like you are taking a breath of fresh air and you will be happier with what you have.

3. Pursue your passion. People who love their life, spend time doing the things they love. If you have a passion that you are not pursuing, then it is clear that you are not happy with what you have. If you don't know what your passion is, looking for it can lead you to feel better about your life. Get used to doing the things you love for as long as possible. Otherwise, if you don't know what you like, spend that time finding it.

If there is nothing pushing you, you will not feel satisfied.

In some cases, you may have the opportunity to turn your passion into a career (as in the case of photography). If that were your case, it would be even more rewarding and would make you particularly happy.

4. Stop aiming for the best. If you want to enjoy your life, you need to know how to be happy with what you have, whether it's a nice home or a wonderful family dinner, instead of always looking for ways to improve your life. Seeking perfection is a "guarantee" of unhappiness; it will make you feel worse and less adequate, regardless of what you have.

As the Rolling Stones said, "You can't always get what you want, but if you try sometimes, you'll get what you need." These are words to remember. Don't obsess about owning the most beautiful things. Focus on being happy with what you have.

Of course, you can always find a better version of anything, be it an Apple device or a new car. Seeking perfection will take you to the end of your strength, making you an eternal miser.

5. Take the time to connect with people. It has been shown that relating to others makes people more fulfilled.

Meaningful relationships are among the most important things in life. They will make you feel less alone and more capable of overcoming problems. Whether you're spending time with your best friend, or chatting with your neighbor, a conversation and interaction, however small, feels better.

Stop offering yourself excuses. Nobody is too busy to have a social life. Try to connect with others at least twice a week.

If there is someone who is especially important to you, don't take them for granted. Take the time to create important memories and to have heartfelt conversations with the one you love.

6. Find time for yourself. Taking a nice warm bath, lighting a scented candle while listening to your favorite music or just lying on the sofa to watch your favorite show are good examples of quality time spent on yourself. These are times when you don't need to spend money, but it's a way to have fun focusing on yourself. Remember that you are important and deserve to be spoiled.

Pampering yourself a little is important and it helps to feel better.

Don't let a friend's improvisation rob you of the time you have reserved for yourself. Protect your time as if you were planning to spend an evening with your favorite star.

7. Make relevant changes in your life if necessary. Of course, changing your outlook and attitude can go a long way in making you happier; but what do you do if there is a real obstacle in your way? If that's the case, you won't be able to enjoy your life if you don't solve the problem. Think long and hard about what stands between you and your happiness. If there is a solution, find a way to put it into practice. Here are some examples:

If you are unhappy because you feel uninspired or unappreciated doing your current job, ask for a promotion, look for something new or think about how to completely change your path.

If you're having a terrible relationship, whether it's the love of your life or a difficult relationship with a close friend, it might be time to cut it off.

If you are particularly overweight and that is holding you back from doing what you would like, it may be time to change your lifestyle by making it healthier.

Part 3: New beginning

1. Help others. Happy people are not only happy with their lives but also love to improve the lives of others. You don't have to work in a canteen, making soup for the homeless if it's not your thing, but you can help others regularly, whether it's by volunteering at a local bookstore, helping a friend study for her math exam, or giving help your younger brother who finds a summer job. Even the little things can make a lot of difference in someone else's life and you will feel happier.

Helping others will make you focus less on yourself and everything you don't have.

2. Love yourself. This is an important factor because you need to be able to love yourself before you can love others. The first step is to get to know you. Determine who you really are and what makes you happy. This will help you love yourself and appreciate the little things in your life.

There is nothing wrong with recognizing your flaws and understanding that you are not perfect. Working to fix as many defects as possible will help you feel better.

3. Try doing something completely new and different than usual. This will open your mind and help you have a less rigid view of life in general. Whether you are learning to cook, taking dance lessons or skydiving, mixing things up will make you feel happier because you will be less focused on your usual methods. Look for a new hobby, go out with a new friend, or just walk to a new place. You will feel happier because they are all ways to change your perspective.

One of the reasons people feel unhappy is the tiredness of doing the same things. Doing at least one completely new thing per week can help you keep an elastic point of view.

4. Enjoy the failures. If you want to be happy, you have to completely fail at something. It can be cooking a complicated pasta dish, organizing a themed party, or making a clay pot. Making mistakes get you used to accepting failures and throwing yourself into new things anyway. Doing badly in front of others also leads you to take yourself less seriously, and consequently, to face life with more irony.

Failing from time to time reminds you that you don't have to be perfect in whatever you try your hands on, and this will undoubtedly make you feel happier.

5. Go out with happy people. If you want to enjoy your life, you need to surround yourself with people who have a good influence on you. They will teach you how to approach life, show you that there are many different ways to be happy, and maybe give you some tips on how to deal with difficult situations. If you surround yourself with people who are always happy, you will be happier yourself.

If you spend all your time with petulant people who are only looking for new reasons to complain about their lives, it will be much more likely that you too will find reasons to be unhappy!

6. Avoid gossip. Gossip and the habit of badmouthing others will make you feel better momentarily, because it allows you to focus on others' problems, but if you were truly happy with your life, you would not need the troubles of others to feel better. In fact, gossip will only fill you with poison, make you look like an untrustworthy person, and bring no real reason to feel better about your life.

Whenever you open your mouth to say something bad about someone, ask yourself if you can say something positive about that person instead. If you can't, don't say anything.

7. Exercise regularly. You may feel too tired or lazy to go to the gym, but you have to put in the effort. Exercising regularly, even if it's only a 20-minute walk to the store, will instantly make you feel happier. Your body will produce endorphins which will help you have a better perspective, giving you more energy for daily activities.

Try to exercise for at least 30 minutes a day, preferably an hour, to feel happier and healthier.

8. Address your personal problems. Happy people know when something is wrong and deal with the situation. Unhappy people let problems escalate until they become unsustainable. If you know you are in a crisis with a family member or friend, try to resolve the conflict and move on with your life, without waiting for the weeks to pass, until you reach the breaking point.

You don't have to clash to have an adult conversation about the things that are bothering you.

At the same time, you should avoid resentment. Don't be angry about what people have done in the past, even if it hurt or bothered you. If that has already passed, move on.

9. Find a purpose in life. Sure, it's easier said than done, but ultimately, it's a habit that sets happy people apart. If you want to enjoy your life and what it offers you, you have to give meaning to your days to make them worth living. It doesn't need to be a career on the rise, all glitter and success. It can be a loving wife, or the joy of being a fantastic part-time teacher. It can be the beautiful rose in your garden, or the chance to travel. Whatever it is, it can excite you every time you wake up, making you happy when you go to bed.

This won't happen overnight, of course. But finding purpose should be one of your life's goals.

CHAPTER 10: Recognize the Importance of Perfect Timing

Time for yourself, time to love and take care of yourself

Take care of yourself, make time for yourself.

Beauty is the ability to identify and enhance oneself. To do this, you need an eye that knows how to look at "everything", at beauty tout court, and draw guidelines to get closer to its purest concept.

It is not mechanical, it is philosophy.

In this chapter, we have drawn up a 4-point ritual dedicated to well-being and beauty.

"Love your neighbor as yourself" means that, in order to be comfortable with others, you must know how to love yourself. Once a day, allow yourself a moment of personal pleasure dedicated to you.

"Feel": Our body, day by day, sends us very clear messages. Don't ignore them. Take four minutes to look in the mirror and ask yourself: "What is my body asking of me?"

"Listen to yourself": Listen to what you have discovered and do not postpone the appointment with your needs. There are many ways to do it: How to follow the Phyto

ritual to love your hair, starting with discovering what they have (and need). Taking the time of beauty.

"*Be loved*": Time spent on oneself is never time lost. Leave all regrets out the door long enough to love you.

All that remains is one last, small, ritual to do: Hold beauty with two hands and enrich it with a pinch of curiosity.

Put yourself at the center. Focus on yourself.

The expression "carve out time" evokes the possibility of indulging in only a fragment of one's day. Let's try to overturn the paradigm then. Instead of talking about "cutting out", let's think about "taking" some time. Sometimes, it takes a little. It may take just ten minutes to feel better, perhaps, with a simple exercise to do at home as soon as you wake up or after returning from work.

"Ten minutes of quiet and ABS": A ritual that comes from Pilates and is dedicated to relaxing the back and toning the abs and buttocks. It can be done as soon as you get home or during your lunch break, to rediscover your breath.

Lie down on the ground. Inhaling widens the ribcage, exhaling "bring the belly in" ten times.

Repeat ten more times, after pushing the lower back down, try to roll the pelvis downwards by performing a retroversion.

"Pampered": Dedicate a few minutes to relax before facing the working delusions of the day once you're at home, after facing a long day of work or after an intense workout.

Spread the body cream and massage carefully, until reaching the face with circular movements and pegs to activate the circulation until it reaches the hair.

Whenever you can dedicate to your favorite ritual, take care of your hair, recreate your beauty salon at home, as Phyto teaches, starting with the pre-shampoo and then moving on to cleansing, rinsing treatment and a pleasant post-rinse treatment. And finally, the styling that will vary according to the mood of the moment. The secret to perfect hair is to follow the complete ritual.

Habits, everyday life and constancy in the execution of gestures make you at peace with yourself. In the long run, every single cell in your body will benefit from your favorite ritual. You will feel more serene, more in harmony and therefore more beautiful.

Be beautiful: If you are relaxed and beautiful on the outside, you are also beautiful on the inside

Read a good book, take time to do only what you like best; whether it is watching a busy talk, a light program, practicing sports or even dedicating time to your beauty. Everything you love to do has a very important value because it relaxes you, makes you happier, at peace with yourself and with others and inevitably makes you look better. The key to everything, therefore, lies in how we are able to manage our mind and body: It is a philosophical approach—just as philosophy is discussed in the Phyto Charter of Values, a creed that was born in the Parisian salons, temples of beauty, where time is the essence of the ritual that is celebrated there, and which speaks precisely of the ability to love yourself. The same love continues in your homes too. The Phyto treatment lines are perfect to use as daily wellness pills in the intimacy of your own spaces.

Now, love yourself and take out some time for you!

Come find inner balance

The secret to feeling good about yourself lies in finding an inner balance in all aspects of yourself, bringing harmony in the body, mind and spirit.

Everything in us is connected, so the balance on the psychological and emotional level, for example, also has repercussions on the body and on our whole being. In fact, when an inner balance is lacking, we experience moments of discomfort, difficulty and pain. Conversely, if we are able to restore the balance between body, mind and spirit, we are able to experience an inner well-being and our life reflects it.

You have to take care of yourself, physically, mentally and inwardly, to restore balance.

Now, I want to talk to you about some aspects you can work on to feel better about yourself.

1. Don't depend on others.
2. Let go of what you don't need.
3. Give up guilt.
4. Abandon judgment.
5. Develop gratitude.
6. Find out who you really are.
7. Discover the dream of your soul.
8. Develop a positive attitude.
9. Let go of limiting beliefs.
10. Do what makes you happy.
11. Open yourself to change.
12. Take care of yourself.

1. Don't depend on others

We must learn to feel good alone and not be emotionally dependent on others. Individual freedom is important, even in couple relationships. In fact, being comfortable with oneself is the condition to be comfortable with others, in any type of relationship. Not depending on others means loving unconditionally, that is, loving without expecting anything in return. It's easy to say, but to do it takes a whole lot.

2. Let go of what you don't need

The people you attract into your life are those who "vibrate" at your own frequency, which you resonate with and who you "need" at that time. But, nothing is forever, so also the people who enter and leave your life. When this happens, you can let go of people or situations that can no longer be a part of your life, without guilt or suffering.

When you change, the people and situations around you also change. Let it be so. Don't get attached to anything or any person.

3. Give up guilt

How often do we accuse ourselves or feel judged by others? We must free ourselves from the sense of guilt that arises when we fall into the traps of the mind. Even if you think you are at fault, you can be able to forgive yourself and develop more self-esteem by trying to transcend the ego.

Appreciating yourself and being able to understand that everything is perfect as it is, is a great leap towards being able to feel good about yourself.

What others think does not have to interest you. The important thing is what you think of yourself. Don't feel judged, rather, understand that you are okay as you are!

4. Abandon judgment

Abandoning judgment on others and on oneself is fundamental. In judging, you do nothing but complain about something that you consider not good. Try to accept the things you cannot change and focus on your inner change.

If you do not like a situation and you cannot change it, do not be damning your soul by being stubborn and raging against yourself, but try to understand why that situation has entered your life and work on what happens on the inside.

Remember that when you point one finger, you have three more pointing towards you!

5. Develop gratitude

Gratitude is one of the best ways to access joy and abundance in our life. We are often distracted by what we don't like in our life and don't pay attention to the small (or big) things to be grateful for every day.

When we develop a deep sense of gratitude, life does nothing but offer us opportunities to be even more grateful for. Try to experience it in your life. What you give comes back to you!

And remember that YOU ARE ALIVE!

6. Find out who you really are

Reconnecting with yourself is a vital step in taking back your power, but first, you need to find out who you really are and take responsibility for your life.

Try to meditate; discover the deepest parts of yourself. Everything you are looking for is within you. Discover your mission in life—that purpose that makes you feel fulfilled, happy, full of enthusiasm, and in deep contact with life.

Being comfortable with yourself is being able to be the best expression of oneself.

7. Discover the dream of your soul

We are able to give our best when we are inspired, when we have this fire inside that pushes us forward.

But what is this force that drives us? Doesn't it arise from our deepest part, from our soul?

Finding the dream of one's soul and pursuing it makes us incredibly happy because we are doing what we truly desire.

Have you ever wondered why you are where you are and what you came to do?

8. Develop a positive attitude

This topic is talked about a lot. Today, science has shown us how thoughts interact with matter.

Our thoughts influence us and the reality that surrounds us; and this bond is very close. Hence, you can understand how important it is to be able to develop a positive inner attitude to positively influence our life.

Controlling your mind, instead of being a slave to it, is important. As a first step, you should understand that energy goes where you put your attention. Learning to "shift" attention from one thought to another is the first step.

Positive thoughts will come by themselves as you work within. The less space you give to your fears, the more you will get used to controlling your mind and creating conscious thoughts of a higher frequency.

Develop a higher thought pattern. To do so, you will need to reconnect to the most authentic part of yourself.

9. Let go of limiting beliefs

The mind, very often, makes us slaves and subjected to patterns and beliefs. It would be good to free yourself from this.

Regaining your power will allow you control your mind and act with greater awareness.

The mind is a very powerful and complex tool. We are often conditioned by limiting beliefs that are rooted in our subconscious. You can transform them by helping yourself with techniques such as Theta Healing; become a co-creator of your reality.

By internally transforming these parts of you that are so deep that they block you, you will see a wonderful transformation happen in your life.

10. Do what makes you happy

Look for what makes you truly happy and eliminate the beliefs that keep you from achieving your dreams.

Oftentimes, what makes us happier is following our passions. This comes from deep within us, but you could be blocking it yourself.

Find a way to express your talents and fulfill your soul's dream. But, remember one important thing: You can be happy now, here, at this very moment.

Happiness is always there; it is we who must re-tune ourselves to the right frequency!

11. Open yourself to change

Everything is constantly changing and flowing in this constant future of our life, allows us to live a more serene life and feel good about ourselves.

If the mind resists, or you are "locked in" patterns and habits, from which you want to break free, develop greater willpower.

Start with small steps. Making even small changes in your life will bring you great results.

If the wind of change is blowing, don't build a wall, but rather, a windmill! - Chinese proverb.

12. Take care of yourself

All aspects of us are important. Taking care of yourself means doing it in all senses.

Try to treat your body in the best way, starting with a healthy diet. Personally, I recommend the vegetarian or vegan one and in any case, the use of natural and organic products for your diet.

If you can, practice some regular movement and activities like Yoga. This benefits both the body and mind.

Today, you can practice many holistic disciplines and vibrational energy techniques, which allow you to work on a more subtle level to restore inner balance.

Surely, you will also find meditation very useful as it is one of the simplest tools, but at the same time, the most effective, to find yourself and achieve a balance between body, mind and spirit.

As an advice, I would tell you that Love is always fundamental. So, love yourself and love! Remember to spend time with the people you love!

Take the time if you want to bloom every day

What does "flourish" mean?

Personal flowering is a different concept from personal growth. While growth spurs us to improve and learn more, flowering contemplates the interior dimension of the person based on his nature, his vocation, and his pace of achievement. Flowering is not a race for improvement at all costs, but a process of realization, during which the inner core that contains the power of one's authentic being slowly blossoms.

It is easy to understand that in this process it is somewhat counterproductive to try to speed up development. Everyone has their own pace. Furthermore, personal flowering does not speak to us of a goal, of an ideal to be achieved, but rather, of something much more concrete: The manifestation of one's identity in all its splendor; it speaks to us of a human, concrete realization, as opposed to an idea of happiness confined to the imagination that we would like to see manifested externally.

When one flourishes, one perceives the change within oneself by feeling that one is aligned with one's being: One no longer engages in violence, trying to be like others or adapting to pre-established norms, but accepts one's uniqueness without fear.

Flowering does not mean chasing an ideal of perfection but rather, welcoming one's nature and developing it from within, moment by moment, with attention to one's well-being, without the performance anxiety typical of personal growth.

"At this point, it becomes extraordinarily easy to understand our life: However we are, we couldn't have been otherwise. No regrets, no wrong paths, no real mistakes. The eye of necessity reveals that what we do is only what could have been. "

(James Hillman)

Flowering is therefore a process that results in one feeling good about oneself and to free the seed of our thousand potentials from everything that blocks it from manifesting itself to the world, or rather "blossom." The question arises: How does it bloom? The answer is simple. Be yourself—fully, unconditionally, without regrets.

In fact, to flourish, it is necessary to welcome one's uniqueness (everyone is different) and to respect each other deeply; this implies knowing one's own needs, choosing to indulge one's talents, respect and improve, not to resemble what one is not, but to get closer and closer to one's authentic being. This step cannot be taken without welcoming and recognizing your flaws.

To flourish means to find the key to beauty deep within oneself, to welcome it and not be afraid to take one's place in the world, to take root and leap upwards.

It is a journey of awareness and manifest-action, of the blossoming of the seed containing our being in potentiality. Through the different stages of inner development, make it manifest to allow its vocation, its action in the world, to spread—because being is the guardian of a vocation.

Personal flowering and the secret of perfume

The allegory of the flower as the meaning of the inner process of realization goes far beyond a purely aesthetic interpretation. If we look closely at this image, we will discover the great wisdom hidden in it.

Unfortunately, thinking about the flowering process, we risk stopping at the image of the flower, which constitutes a stage and not the goal of the allegory, thinking that the realization in the beauty of one's being is the ultimate end of the authentic being enclosed within us. There is more.

It is true that reaching the stage of being in which one's nature and uniqueness is manifested is an important stage that is not easy to reach, but we risk forgetting the function and purpose of flowering. In the flower, there is an invisible, but at the same time, fundamental dimension, without which it would not be able to be totally itself. It contains an extremely important symbol: Perfume.

What does the perfume represent? In the collective unconscious, the perfume refers to the sacred dimension. In religious rites and temples, it was associated with divinity, because it was associated with the breath of life. The nose, the sensory organ capable of perceiving the scent is directly connected to the brain, to the point of representing a bridge between the internal dimension and the external world. Due to its ability to communicate with the brain and the unconscious in particular, the sense of smell (the first sense developed, and connected to an ancient part of the brain) is able to awaken our memory, but perhaps the most interesting and forgotten perfume is to be a message—a bridge between the unconscious of two people or more.

In the allegory of personal flowering, those who bloom unconsciously send a message around them. But, for what purpose? Perfume, as previously mentioned, has always been connected to the sacred dimension of being, to Pneuma, to the breath of life; the metaphorical "perfume" emanating from a person who has achieved his own flowering conveys a message of inspiration to those around him, sending a message of hope: "Spring is near, remember who you are."

Who knows, maybe it's the flowers that make the spring...

By now, we all agree: This era is voracious of time, it uses it all and does not allow you to dedicate time to it.

We could go in depth and read all the facets of this sentence. When faced with a more accurate analysis, you often realize that you don't want to take this time, that you fill it with something else. Of everything!

It seems that dedicating yourself to yourself is often something frightening, which highlights your weaknesses, forces you to confront who you are, what you want and what you do. This is frightening.

I am convinced that this is not so horrible. It will certainly have uncomfortable, perhaps, unwanted moments, but taking time for yourself can only help you flourish, get to know you, understand you and therefore be more aware of what you do and what you choose.

"Okay, so what do I do? I lie down on the sofa and think?"

If I did that, I'd be asleep in less than five minutes. My time would surely be appreciated by my eternal sleepiness, but of little use to introspection.

Decide a day and an hour when YOU choose what to do. You have to choose what to do by FEELING what you want, what you FEEL you need, FEEL you miss, FEEL that will make you happy.

It's your thing: A walk, a cake, a phone call, a book, a trip, a bath, a massage—away from "everything else" (cell phone, internet, work etc.)

As you do it, realize that you are doing it and enjoy it.

This is also a way to satisfy your needs, from the most banal to the most stringent ones.

Ignoring what you need makes you unsatisfied, sad, and apathetic.

We must regain the freedom to choose what really matters to us, in order to be better and happier people.

Take the time to learn to feel good about yourself too.

Introspection is something powerful!

Perhaps, due to personal vicissitudes, I often find myself looking within. I have learned that honesty towards oneself is a good start to understanding what we think and the mechanisms that trigger certain situations. Understanding why we feel like this certainly helps us to get out of certain mental loops that are typical of this era. For example, I'm talking about the deception of social media, which misinforms us by proposing unreal realities. Or of this frantic rush to possess things, not even those that qualify us in society, and how it makes us feel inadequate, inferior or envious.

Looking inside is useful for me to understand what I don't like in my life and instead of fretting, I try to change what I don't like. If I can't change it, I have to understand that it's part of what I have to carry with me. I won't be able to enjoy it, but I can't be perpetually angry or sad about something I can't change, about several things that do not suit me, but have to keep, things I could've changed! In the end, all of this makes me feel more peaceful. This reasoning leads to another concept: We are all different and unique.

Take the time to know your needs, to indulge your talents. This will allow you to free yourself from the rush of being like others or better than others, but to be more you—more authentic and happier.

Being happy undoubtedly improves your relationship with the world around you; be it family, friends or work.

CHAPTER 11: How Not to Suffer from Loneliness?

The solution is within you.

Emotional Independence

In this chapter, I want to talk to you about how to stop suffering from loneliness.

Almost everyone is convinced that to overcome loneliness, it is necessary to be together with others, to have a relationship as a couple (which is fundamental!), to have many friends, go out, and be around people.

Hardly does anyone think about loneliness as an emotional problem. It is actually the paradoxical consequence of our constant search for the things we believe we need.

One of the many paradox of our society is that we are always in contact, we can stay connected with others wherever we are.

We can reach any point in the world in a very short time, we are always among people, we have many friends and many acquaintances. Forming new relationships has never been so simple, yet we are capable of suffering loneliness equally, feeling alone even while in contact with many people.

You may have experienced those moments when you feel sad and lonely, or alone, when things really don't seem to go the right way, when others can't understand and help you.

A profound inner loneliness, often difficult for others to understand. Or maybe you live with people who often feel this way. It all depends on our emotions.

Before I tell you how to eliminate loneliness, take a few minutes to take my emotions test.

It will allow you to understand how to eliminate suffering from your life.

Maybe you are among those who are convinced that life cannot reserve happiness for us, that being happy is an illusion or a deception, and that after all we are all alone, because everyone, more or less, always has an ulterior motive.

Today, let's dispel all these myths and I'll explain how to defeat loneliness forever.

Suffering from loneliness is not a social problem

One of the strongest fears we feel in our life is that of being alone, certainly not of being able to isolate yourself for a moment in your room, away from the chaos of everyday life, but of being marginalized and isolated from others.

We are afraid of being excluded because we feel we cannot do without others, we are afraid of suffering without a partner, of not being able to live happily without friends or acquaintances with whom to spend time.

We are afraid of loneliness, that being alone means not being loved, that is, living a life poor in love.

I will tell you what I have learned, experienced in my own skin and seen many people live: Even if no one loves you, your happiness would never be precluded, if not by your belief that without others who love you, you will be alone and suffering.

We can be fine alone, but the most important thing is to understand that when you get to this, you will hardly be isolated.

All negative emotions come from fear. Fear is the basis of every negative emotion, and it is the one we feel most often, without recognizing it.

- ✓ Friends who, if they have no interest in being with us, go away.
- ✓ Partners who take another path if we don't meet their needs.
- ✓ People who are part of our "company" only because they gain something.

Perhaps you too, if you do not find satisfaction in others, leave them alone and take a different path.

But this simply means that these relationships never gave or created love, but were a simple exchange of interest.

Better to be alone at this point.

Hypocrisy, on the other hand, does not like anyone, but nobody totally rejects it.

The fear of being alone is a problem for those who do not know how to live without Linus crutches and blankets capable of giving them the security that they cannot find within themselves.

I am convinced that loneliness is not a bad thing, on the contrary, it is a fundamental step to learn to love, to know each other, to discover who we really are and to be able to get in touch with the most authentic version of ourselves.

Solitude is that space in which we find the tranquility to reflect and grow. The big problem is that today, we are scared of it. Suffering from loneliness is often the consequence of a constant flight to the outside.

We anesthetize the inner voice, we ignore the contradictions that characterize us, and we silence our true nature by any means.

We surround ourselves with people, we overburden ourselves with commitments and appointments, we always find new ways to "have fun" and we do everything possible to ensure that we are always around people. To combat loneliness, many resort to the use of alcohol, or drugs; others spend hours in front of video games and television.

Many seek contact with others, with the belief that they will feel less lonely if they are surrounded by other people.

Others plunge into a relationship, or enter and leave relationships that are more or less sentimental, if not exclusively sexual.

We run away from ourselves but we must admit, however, that it is useless.

In the end we have to be alone (which is different from feeling alone!) We have to find out who we.

We run away because we don't like to suffer and we have been taught that we will suffer if we are alone.

We are convinced that those who spend a long time alone are not well and have some problems.

This is a misconception. To overcome loneliness, we must first understand it.

Being alone does not mean being isolated; we are afraid of isolation, of the distancing that others may impose on us, of being excluded.

We confuse loneliness with the exclusion imposed on us by others, and therefore we try to escape from this alleged prison.

The first thing to understand is that loneliness is positive and fundamental for your life. If we are not able to feel good alone, without needing someone always with us, we will never be able to feel good even with others.

If we learn to be with ourselves, to appreciate the silence of a dawn without anyone to distract us, if we begin to dedicate real time to reflect, if we learn to know each other and love solitude, we will no longer be afraid of it and we will not suffer.

You can overcome this fear by carving out time every day just for yourself, without artificial distractions (books, television, and cell phones).

There is no need to disappear for hours. A little time away is enough, as long as it is not occupied by anything other than the moment itself. In reality, no one can suffer from loneliness, only abstinence; abstinence from all forms of "distraction" that we use in order not to be alone with ourselves.

When we have learned to love solitude, we can love company, without needing it. When we get rid of the need of people, as De Mello also says, then we can love them.

In order not to suffer from loneliness, we must learn to love and understand it. From here, we will learn to be free and to truly love, because loneliness is not the absence of others, but the presence of ourselves.

I remember a poem I read several years ago, whose author and title escape me. It says:

> *"...among so many people feeling alone, in so much light being in the dark, in great celebration feeling absent."*

I hope I quoted these verses correctly, but the thing I care about is that loneliness is not overcome by the chaos around us. Suffering from loneliness is the result of a bad relationship with ourselves.

Of course, we do not consciously make such a decision, but if we do not begin to realize that the sadness we feel, as well as the loneliness and emptiness we feel, are our responsibility, something we produce in our life, we will never be able to get out of it.

Emotional independence is a crucial step in getting rid of negative emotions that become a limit to our life.

Sadness is the fruit of our stubborn repulsion for reality. We refuse that things do not go our way.

When we are resigned to seeing our dreams broken, we become sad, because we are convinced that the situation cannot improve. We remain in a state of immobility, without desire to do, without the ability to love and smile.

We wallow in our troubles and misfortunes, intensifying the sadness, because we keep thinking that things should have been different.

Being sad is up to me.

Loneliness is a fake fear, or rather, it is not something natural, but the fruit of the convictions that our society transmits. In many cultures, being alone becomes a frequent and fundamental experience to get to know yourself better, a means of self-care. .

In ours, it is often avoided as if it were a disease, and we ask those on the sidelines if they are sick!

Loneliness is the only time we can discover who we really are. There is no happy life that is not spiced with so many moments of loneliness.

Once again, it is we who, unable to live autonomously and independently from an emotional point of view, end up being afraid of loneliness, the lack of others and the silence that brings us the responsibility of our life.

Where to begin to defeat loneliness then?

First, we must understand that loneliness is a friend and not a threat, exploiting it to begin to know ourselves, to understand what makes us sad, to understand our thoughts and emotions.

From this knowledge, we can begin to notice how sadness arises when we make claims, and we can always starting from the calm of loneliness to get rid of them.

Sadness disappears if we choose happiness, if we decide to live with love and learn to love in an authentic way.

If we want to be happy, it is not the love of others that we need (and that often pushes us to beg for their company), but to actively give love.

Loving must be our way of life, the way we observe the world, the way we interact with anyone, including ourselves. If I really love, I can only love myself. But can I say that I love someone I can't be alone with?

If you can't stay an hour or a whole day with your friend, could you say you love him, or feel good about it? If you can't be alone with you, it's the same. The problem is not if the others are not there, the problem is if you manage to live with joy, every moment of solitude. We usually want to spend time with the people we say we love, we want to give them attention, share experiences, and get to know them better.

Yet, paradoxically, we are often unable to love ourselves, the only person who has been and will always be present in our life.

We don't really love if we don't love ourselves, and being afraid of loneliness means being afraid of finding out who we are, of being alone with ourselves. A person who cannot feel good alone has not learned to love himself and therefore, he has not learned to love others either, at most he will be able to indulge them in order to have the company he believes is indispensable.

We can defeat loneliness by opening our eyes, learning that it is a fundamental space to grow, to improve, to learn to love.

We are afraid of loneliness to the extent that we do not love and expect others to make us feel good.

We are afraid of loneliness because we believe that our happiness depends on the presence of others.

We are afraid of loneliness because we do not look at reality and we do not realize, that no measure of our happiness depends on others.

If we need them, we will not love, and paradoxically we will be surrounded by many people, but our life will still be loveless.

What a sad result!

Better to be alone than not learning to love and making love the center of our life.

Remember that love and fear are never close. If you fear loneliness, you will not choose love because you are afraid. It takes courage to love— to change and choose life.

We must not be afraid of being alone, but of being unable to love, even for just another day of our life.

Emotional independence is a fundamental aspect to overcome loneliness, to free ourselves from the dependence on others, which denies us the possibility to love authentically and be happy.

Start from this; start creating the happiness you want, even in moments of solitude. To do this, start applying the 10 secrets of positive emotions.

Only if you know how to be happy alone, can you be happy with others.

Everything depends on you.

Chapter 12: Recognize the Importance of the Perfect Moment When You Are Single

Being single is a symbol of power, let's claim it

"Are you swiping?" My best friend asks me for breakfast one morning. I swallow a spoonful of sadly, tasteless porridge and think for a moment how to respond.

The answer is no, I wasn't swiping. But as I told him, I found myself in a bewildered expression. In this period, I really don't want to slide my finger on a screen, or even hang out with anyone, because since I started dating guys at 15, in every relationship, I have had the same, unpleasant pattern, made up of unbalanced power relationships.

Now, my status as an inveterate single is now consolidated, following the countless and prolonged breaks I have taken between one relationship and another—not because I don't like the idea of being in a relationship, but because I find it very tiring to date someone. Let's face it clearly: It is universally known that dating someone is not always a walk in the park, for anyone. But, as a woman who dates men, all the relationships I've had—from casual sex to long, committed relationships—have turned out to be a long way from the idea of equality I had imagined I could experience in a relationship. Having no say in my love life has led me to want to stay single, in order to hold on to some semblance of control. To avoid that feeling of helplessness, I have chosen not to date anyone.

It strikes me that even today—despite the new wave of feminism—not having a partner makes me almost an anomaly, an exception for my friends and my family. For decades, we have been trying to change the stereotype of the sad and melancholy single spinster, to bring it closer to reality: An independent woman, capable of choosing, who resists the pressures of a patriarchal society and the values we have inherited from it. But, did it work? The way I see it, the pressures that Bridget Jones and Carrie Bradshaw felt in the 1990s and 2000s are the same pressures that still prevail today.

In every type of relationship that I have had, at every stage, I have had to deal with unbalanced power relationships and misogynistic microaggressions. The last serious relationship I had was with a guy who used sexist insults at me—"slut", "crazy", "sick"—when I tried to assert myself or expressed dissatisfaction with something. He spoke openly about my friends, considering them objects, commodifying their appearance. I ditched him, vowing to be more selective with my next mate.

The one I went out with next would get impatient when I spoke and would say, "Come on, Rachel," if I asked him questions about topics I didn't know much about. The world of online dating has its pains, with matches that insistently ask you to send naked photos of you, photos of cocks/ penises that arrive unsolicited, with intimidation and offense if you take too long to reply to a message or refuse a message.

My sexual experiences with men have been characterized by a net imbalance of forces that left me vulnerable, traumatizing me at times. When I look back at certain encounters from the past, from a *#MeToo* perspective, I realize that a worrying percentage of my sexual encounters lie in what I would call a gray area—sex that is not illicit, but can be perceived as violence. I felt compelled to do things, I felt pain and violence during sex, experiencing it as a trauma. I once asked the guy I was having sex with to stop because I had changed my mind. He started yelling at me with a slew of insults, until my roommate stepped in and helped me get rid of him.

For a heterosexual woman, dating someone is even more complicated, because the male gender, to which we are attracted, exercises a systematic control over us.

Maybe it's my fault, maybe it's me who's wrong to choose men, I've told myself countless times. To fix this, I also revised my partner selection criteria. A few years ago, I swore to only go out with men who claimed to be feminists. This path brought a lot of other problems, first of them being the "performative wokeness", a false sensibility of the facade. This definition, which has recently become part of the common lexicon, refers to people who publicly say they believe in social justice, that they are on the side of women, people of color, LGBTQ people and people with disabilities. The experiences I have had with men who claimed to be feminists lead me to say that their behavior, when we were together, was not in line with the values they claimed to follow. Privately, there have been several forms of microaggression, from gaslighting to deviously paternalistic attitudes that have made me question my sanity.

In reality, there's a lot more to it than just picking the kind of guy I can like. Blythe Roberson, writer and comic writer, author of "How to Date Men When You Hate Men", says that dating is difficult for everyone, but "for a straight woman, dating is even more complicated because the male gender we are attracted to affects a systematic control of us."

"It can be obvious, or manifest in more subtle ways, which I have often ignored, like when a man says he would never go out with a woman who is more successful than he is, or he considers me superficial because I deal and write about love affairs, etc."

---

says Roberson.

They think 'I'm fucking this, but I'm not taking it home to meet mom and dad.'

My experience, of course, is not representative of all men, nor of all women. A transwoman dating a man faces another set of problems, the chief problem being sexually appreciated but not respected.

Paris Lees, a columnist for British Vogue and an activist committed to raising awareness on trans issues says, there are men who enjoy having sex with trans women but are ashamed to seriously date them. "It's interesting to see that when you tell a guy you're trans, he immediately goes 'Oh, then I can't even help but respect you.'" Many young people, although not all, think 'I'm going to fuck this one, but I won't take it home to meet mum and dad'".

Lees is convinced that discussions about whether or not trans women are "real women" have exacerbated the misogyny towards them. "At the height of the debate that dominated the British media months ago—'Are trans women real women?'—I had to deal with a man who treated me very badly and I remember thinking: 'What a joke'", says Lees. "Seriously, they tell me that I'm not a real woman and then I find myself here getting all these misogynistic attacks."

Indiana Seresin, a scholar specializing in feminist and queer theory, is convinced that, "dating people of the opposite sex is often tiring for a woman."

"Having to deal with the sense of male legitimacy, the unfair division of physical and emotional workloads, and men's ignorance of female sexuality is exhausting," Seresin tells me. "As a queer woman, I can safely say that we don't have to deal with many of these problems, thank God. On the other hand, there are still a number of cultural norms that we have sadly inherited from heterosexuality, one of which is the model, same as a couple."

Redefine the stereotype of the single woman

The hegemony of the couple is something that we, as a society, struggle to free ourselves from. It prevents us from evaluating what it means to give up traditional schemes, deciding, for example, not to want to see anyone. If we think back to popular culture single girls—Jane Eyre, Elizabeth Bennett, Carrie Bradshaw, Bridget Jones, Kat Stratford—their stories all end with a happy ending, when they find Mister Right. It always ends with these petulant intellectuals finding the cure for their ills—this cure being a man. I don't want this medicine and I'm also sure I'm not sick.

If women have greater economic autonomy, attempting to embarrass them because they want to remain single is just a way for patriarchy to control them.

This idea that single women need to be treated is really frustrating for Maria Del Russo, a writer who deals with sex and wellness. "It seems to me that among women, there is still a widespread idea that 'single' is a negative condition and not yet another label that society wants to stick on you," Del Russo tells me. "If a woman is single, then something is wrong and she needs to be treated. There's this idea that singles have something wrong, and it's just wrong. "

Not only do we think single women are "broken" people who need to be "fixed", but there is also the stereotype of the "sad single girl" (think of Bridget Jones in her pajamas on the sofa singing "All by Myself" by Céline Dion).

Roberson says there is "certainly the stereotype of the sad single or the frustrated single"—a label she thinks she has also put on her. "I think a lot of people have associated my book title and sentimental status with the fact that I was, like incel, unwittingly single," he explains, laughing.

Don't denigrate women who don't go out with anyone.

Dating someone shouldn't be considered a mandatory exam in life's graduate program. According to Roberson, the fact that women "have easier access to education, work, contraception, abortion and divorce means that they do not have to structure their existence in relation to a man."

> "So, if women have more autonomy economically, trying to embarrass them because they want to stay single is just a way for the patriarchy to control them."

This humiliation can manifest itself in an attitude that Seresin calls "feigned concern", which many singles know well. Think of all the times someone looked at you, tilting their head to the side, and said "come on, you'll find someone" or "you have a soulmate somewhere too" when you say you're single.

"The woman who gives up dating someone is denigrated by our culture (even with 'false worry')," explains Seresin. "It is important to read it as proof that this is a radical choice."

"Our society is still terrified of women who come to the conclusion that they don't need a heterosexual partner," she continues. "Most of the novels of this literary genre feature worlds that have developed technologies to allow reproduction in the absence of man and in which one realizes that, all of a sudden, the male contribution to society is literally zero".

When a woman says she is single and happy, believe her.

As women who have no children are stigmatized, we are also led to consider single women as tragic figures who need solidarity and not worthy of admiration. In some cases, social conditioning tends to make us question our happiness as single. Lees points out the contradiction between how she views other single women and how she experiences her being single.

"Deep down, if I have to tell the truth, I never believed those who say they are happily single," explains Lees. "I have been for a year and I am really happy. So, does that mean I can't believe what I'm experiencing in person?"

Lees even came to think that her happiness was something she convinced herself to feel. But, at Christmas she took stock of her life said to herself: "No, maybe you are really happy, Paris."

Think of the single icons that society promotes

Pop culture celebrates singles, but we must pay attention to the weight of the racial element in what we believe to be the standard bearers of the "singles by choice" movement. "Everyone goes crazy for Rihanna, saying she's not looking for a man, or for that video where Eartha Kitt bursts out laughing at the idea of compromising for a man."

"They are both phenomenal, and I totally agree, but in my opinion, we need to reflect on the fact that our culture puts black women in the role of patron saint of singles, because they have always been excluded from the traditional tale of romantic couple life."

"In romantic comedies, for example, there is the character of the single 'cheeky' black woman who is best friends with the white girl who eventually conquers the man. Making Rihanna or Eartha Kitt the spokespersons for the rejection of heterosexual couple life means forcing them to play the same role."

Historically, the single black woman has always been disparaged. In the 1960s, the Moynihan Report—a study of black families compiled during the presidency of Lyndon B. Johnson—essentially blamed black women for the crisis of the traditional family model. In 1976 and 1980, Ronald Reagan fomented racist rhetoric by using the term "welfare queens"—a label historically used for single, black women, as a bugbear against social security exploitation. Now that our culture is slowly changing its mind about the desirability of single women, it is important to recognize that the black woman as a scapegoat is our cultural heritage.

Consider the relationship a side dish, not the main dish

It's hard not to think about love affairs as the theme is omnipresent in mainstream culture. Love is on television, in the pages of the books we read, in our Instagram feed, and is a topic of discussion with our friends. We may not be able to do much to get rid of this general fixation on love, but we can at least try to reconsider the importance we as individuals place on relationships.

Del Russo, a writer who deals with sex and wellness, says that, "Until the culture changes and they stop making us believe that the love relationship is the ultimate goal to aspire to, we must begin to change our attitude."

"I started thinking of relationships like a scented candle (Follow me). Is it a nice accessory that improves the environment? Sure. But, is the environment complete even without the scented candle? Of course!"

To start changing attitudes about relationships and the importance we attach to them, ask yourself questions: "Why do I want to be in a relationship? What do I think I can get from a relationship that I am not able to achieve alone?"

The weight of society's anxieties should never fall on the shoulders of a single woman. "No one can change things alone—there cannot be a revolution if it is only one woman doing it".

What we, as individuals, can do is question our preconceptions about love relationships; for example, the idea that a single woman cannot be happy alone, or that even our most famous single icons will one day give in to love.

With or without love, I know I'm already complete like this and that's the only thing that matters to me.

Chapter 13: How to Grow Professionally to Advance Your Career (And Your Business)

Many think that professional growth is only the result of job promotions, leading to higher income. Yes, this is probably the right recognition for having developed new skills and competences, but to grow professionally in a concrete way, you first need individual development. It means investing in your training and then putting it into practice in everyday life and work.

If you invest in your personal and professional development, you will see many benefits, including new career and business opportunities, as well as the ability to fill roles in greater prestige. Nowadays, more and more people are committed to acquiring the skills necessary to find a rewarding job, or with the aim of achieving success. In fact, growing professionally does not only allow you to make a career within your company or as a freelancer. A higher professional level allows you to develop and grow your business and make your brand stronger in the eyes of consumers.

Are you wondering what the connection is between these two things? Don't worry, I'll explain everything to you in this chapter.

Man is naturally designed to evolve and improve over time, but then why don't all men manage to achieve their goals?

It happens because not all human beings are constant over time. Education and the future are based on planning and commitment, as well as creativity and opportunity. That's exactly what I want to talk to you about today.

The path to achieving your professional goals intersects with your personal development. Today, we see how you can grow professionally and change your fortunes by following a series of steps. You are primarily responsible for your success!

What do professional growth and personal development mean?

Personal development and professional growth are closely related. The development of one encourages and depends on the other and vice versa. Growing professionally means that you need to focus on acquiring skills and abilities that will have a positive impact on your current job. That is to say that you will get promotions in the workplace or that you will develop the skills you need to make a positive change in your business.

By expanding your skills, your professional figure will stand out more in your current place of work. You will also be in greater demand by other employers. Professional growth leads to an increase in your earning potential and allows you to continue on your path, without remaining stagnant.

No matter what your current position is, there is always something new you can learn or improve on to get more positive results.

On the other hand, growing professionally is a process that remains an end in itself, if it is not also supported by personal development. By knowing how to improve yourself, you will also be able to evolve individually. This is the only way to manage your fears, take responsibility and succeed when you face your challenges. Investing in your personal and professional growth is a demonstration of ambition, awareness and tenacity. These qualities will help you get what you want in both life and work.

Why is it important to grow professionally?

In general, professional growth is important in order to achieve satisfactory work goals.

From the moment we are passing through a constantly evolving labor and trade market, the growth of professional figures becomes essential to support the transformation of the business.

Keeping yourself updated on the trends and directions that technology and sales techniques are taking, allows you to have greater competitive advantages over your competitors.

But who are your competitors?

All other individuals who aspire to have your job or whatever you want are your competitors. In addition, entrepreneurial and professional figures more prepared for new challenges will be able to advance their businesses today and in the years to come. If you have a business, you will have realized how things have changed. The professions and tools of today didn't even exist before, everything advances quickly.

You will be able to keep up with change only if you continue to grow both professionally and personally.

You must first develop the mental resilience that allows you to cope with change and be more resilient even within the business world. If you take care of your personal development, you will be ready to face the professional one too, and consequently, you will have in your deck the right cards to grow your business today.

Are you wondering where to start? I'll give you some that you can put into practice immediately, day after day.

To be able to grow professionally, you have to have a purpose. By having a clear goal, you can you find the right motivation that will give you the boost you need to build your career growth plan.

The objectives can be multiple:

- ✓ Keep your job
- ✓ Earn more
- ✓ Make a career in your company
- ✓ Get the place you've been wanting for a while
- ✓ Change profession
- ✓ Start your own business
- ✓ Grow the company you own

In addition to these, there are many other reasons that can push you to want to grow to get better and more. What all these objectives have in common is that they need concrete actions and are carried out over time in order to be realized.

Tips for growing professionally

1. Focus on long-term goals

You probably already have your list of goals to work on, but are you sure they are structured effectively? To achieve better results, you need to set long-term goals and then chart your way through many short-term goals. It's the same process. Who uses leaders to build their successful businesses? You must have in mind the ultimate cause, the ultimate goal you want to achieve. This is equivalent to your "why", that is, it is the reason that drives you to want to make the leap in professional quality. In order to achieve what you have set for yourself, you must set all those short-term goals to work on daily. In this way, step by step, you will learn everything you need and that leads you to be ever closer to the final result.

Having long-term goals is useful for not losing sight of direction and for having the general picture of what you have and what you still need. Short-term goals are useful for feeling first-hand, the progress you make. They help you stay focused on the road to your goal.

2. Make a plan

One of the best and most profitable ways to develop yourself and your career is to make sure you keep learning. Unfortunately, it is possible and very frequent to lose sight of the goal. Life is made up of many things and distractions are everywhere. Of course, you can change your mind and change your goals. The important thing is to do it voluntarily and consciously.

Don't let your fulfillment be due to chance or events. To complete your project, you have to prepare a training program, you have to make commitments and stick to them. If you need to, mark it as a commitment for your training hours on a diary or as a reminder on your smartphone.

Study and learn the things you need to achieve your goal.

If you know what you want to achieve, it will also be easier to know what you need to do to gain the skills and experience you need.

3. Accept constructive criticism

It is important to know how to handle criticism in a healthy way. You know what they say: "The first step to solving a problem is to admit it exists."

The same thing goes for being able to grow professionally. You have to admit that there are things you still don't know, things you can learn or can do better, so accept the comments and advice of those who are better prepared than you on a particular topic and treasure the suggestions you receive.

There won't always be people willing to give you constructive criticism, to tell you exactly where you need to improve. Most of the time, you will have to experience it firsthand and understand in the field, what works and what doesn't. What you have to do is also learn from your mistakes because that's where you find the key to take a further step on the ladder, towards the achievement of your goals.

Today, we talk about the growth mindset, the mentality that predisposes you not to stop in front of difficulties, but to always find a solution.

Therefore, turn your eyes and ears to valuable feedback and forget, the comments from people who don't want to help you. Accept only the opinions that help you improve as a person and as a professional.

When it comes to career development, it also helps to discuss your plans with your supervisor or your mentor—someone you respect and who has already experienced the path you want to take.

Both of these figures can help you clarify your ideas and set the short-term goals we talked about earlier and that will get you to your final goal.

4. Develop new skills

Your professional growth must certainly be accompanied by the study and development of new skills. You generally have to move in two ways:

1. Improve what you already know by aiming to be the best in your field.
2. Learn what you don't yet know but need and help you do your job even better.

The important thing is that everything you do must make sense and be focused on your goal. If you learn many disparate things, you will have too varied skills that will not be able to contribute to the growth of your professional figure.

So, consider what you need carefully and leave everything else as a hobby in your free time. Imagine your professional growth as the structure of a building: Start from the foundations, move on to the load-bearing and indispensable walls, then continue with the walls, the floors, ceilings, main rooms, fixtures and then move on to interior design to embellish everything. Each element must be in harmony with everything else, otherwise your project will not be achievable in the end.

5. Take advantage of what you learn

Learning does not end when you have finished studying the lesson. The best way to make your skills concrete is to bring what you have studied into your reality. This way, you can discover if you have understood it correctly and if it really works. Many of the things you learn, you must apply to your specific situation. There is a need for a moment of experimentation and consolidation of knowledge. You quickly forget what you do not use. For this reason, the time frame between theory and practice should be short. .

What if you don't have opportunities to put your new knowledge into practice?

Well, you can't wait for things to happen to you, create your opportunities yourself.

If you work in a company, you propose news yourself, while if the company is yours, involve your collaborators in your idea and work with it. In fact, another great way to consolidate your skills, is to teach them to someone else. This puts you in a position to be on the side of the one who is more experienced and to set your mind in motion more productively.

6. Take on your challenges

To really grow professionally, you need to learn to bring challenges in line with your level of preparation, which means that, to improve your performance, you have to do jobs that are possible but challenging for you.

They shouldn't be too easy tasks, otherwise you won't put in a lot of effort to accomplish them, but they shouldn't be too hard to achieve. The right challenges are those that take you off the famous comfort zone. In the process of overcoming these challenges, you develop everything you need to deal with them.

It works just like physical training: To develop muscles, you always have to lift weights that are a little bigger than what you are used to. You have to bring the muscle under stress, but it must be an effort that you can make, albeit with commitment and determination. Always give something more, do your best, keep your focus on the task you have to do. Above all, always tackle your challenges.

Conclusion

Always remember that to grow professionally, you must also think about your personal development. Only in this way will you be ready for all the responsibilities that professional growth entails. Furthermore, set long-term goals on which all the choices you make along the way depend. This applies to career advancement and the development of your business; the approach to be applied is the same.

In both cases, you must be clear about the final result, stay focused, prepare a program to follow to reach the goal, develop new skills in line with your goal, put into practice what you study, learn from your mistakes and face all your challenges. If you need a hand to clarify your ideas, ask for help from those who have been there before you, who can give you some good advice. This is also a way to grow as a person and as a professional.

CHAPTER 14: Positive Mental Attitude

Thinking positive, the art of smiling at life

Seeing the glass half full, considering things lightly, learning the right lessons from your mistakes and being indulgent towards those of others is important. A positive attitude helps you feel better about yourself and others.

That of "positive thinking" is an attitude, a way of relating to life and the events that happen. The basic concept is simple. Every event of our existence involves an emotional reaction on our part and this reaction has the ability to affect our mood, conditioning other events and relationships with people.

Learning to always look for the positive side of things is an attitude that has the power to influence our state of mind. There are studies and disciplines that teach positive thinking and training to maintain this condition. Neurolinguistic programming, for example, teaches how to modulate language (towards others but also towards ourselves) which will then be able to influence our way of considering things. Not having the power to influence the happening of events, all we can work on is our reaction to them happening.

Is positive thinking enough to feel good?

It has been shown that there are close connections between emotions and health. Stress, the scientific community agrees, can cause illness and a negative and anxious attitude can worsen physical or mental conditions and even weaken our immune system. However, it is important not to fall into easy simplifications that can lead to believing that positive thinking can replace medicine or prevention. Although it is proven that it helps, and in some cases, it is fundamental, positive thinking is something to consider as a good habit, a way to smile at life and at others, to learn to draw lessons from everything that happens to us, allowing us respond well to a negative diagnosis and to respond better to treatment.

-

Mental Exercises to Train You to Think Positive

History has shown us on several occasions that those who have a positive outlook to life are also those who generally achieve the most success.

There is no shortage of quotes from great entrepreneurs on the importance of positive thoughts and an optimistic mental attitude.

Personally, changing my mental attitude from negative to learning to think positively has involved a radical change in my lifestyle, both personally and professionally.

The change of mental approach, veering towards positive thinking, has involved passing from a series of failures and states of depression.

"Today is the result of yesterday's thoughts, tomorrow will be the result of today's thoughts."

As the Americans say, "Sharing means caring."

You will find below, some tips that have helped me to eliminate the negative mentality and make the positive prevail.

Learning how to think positively is possible, let's see how to do it together.

Exercises for the mind: How to think positive? Express gratitude!

One of the simplest ways to increase your positivity is to express gratitude.

Being aware and grateful for what you have in the present involves an immediate release of the negativity that you may be holding onto without even realizing it. Gratitude immediately puts you in touch with the feeling of love.

Where love resides, fear and other negative emotions fail to take root.

The best and most effective way to start this mechanism in your life is to express gratitude every morning.

Upon awakening, think about ten things you are grateful for, ten positive aspects of your life—no matter how small or big these things are—whether they are valid only for you or universally recognizable.

This list can be thought out within the confines of your mind, or spoken aloud, but it must be detailed and must come from your heart.

Closing your eyes can be of greater help in this practice.

Many times, negative thoughts arise from the fact that we are too focused only on the negative aspects of our life. You can shift these feelings by unconditionally giving to others.

Share your skills with the people around you. If anyone is looking for advice, help them. Do not hesitate and do not doubt your worth. Even the smallest of shared gestures or thoughts can cause a huge change in another individual's perspective.

Check your breathing.

It is said that those who have the ability to control their breathing have the ability to control their life. In many respects, this statement is quite true.

Think of past occasions when you have lost control. What was happening to your way of breathing? In a fit of anger and anxiety, your breathing becomes short and fast.

By controlling your breath, you can understand and change negative emotions by replacing them with pure positive energy.

In a quiet place, or during the exercise of one of the techniques of relaxation which we have already spoken, try to follow your breath and conscious.

As you inhale (through your nose) try to feel the air entering your body and flowing down to your lungs, feel it as it slowly leaves your body (through your mouth) as you exhale and release all tension with it.

Visualize success.

Tapping into your ability to visualize and imagine can be used as a powerful tool to become more positive.

Many famous people and the undoubted success, such as Oprah Winfrey, Will Smith, Tiger Woods and Arnold Schwarzenegger are known for their ability to visualize what they want to achieve in their lifetime.

Why shouldn't you be able to focus on positive thoughts about life?

Start by closing your eyes. Think of a positive event that happened to you in the past. Your mind can visualize the event in question exactly as it happened.

Put yourself in the middle of that event and focus on the positive emotions that you have marked. When you open your eyes, allow yourself to remain in that positive state of mind. The effects of visualization become amplified with constant practice.

Meditate.

Meditation, among the exercises for the mind, is one of the most effective ways to increase your positivity.

The practice of meditation techniques expands awareness within the individual and allows one to establish a connection between mind, body and soul.

Through meditation techniques and exercises, you can learn to get rid of the negative emotions that drag you down, by connecting to your inner self.

Find a quiet, comfortable place to sit, lie down, or put yourself in any position you feel comfortable in, starting the mental exercises. Close your eyes, take a few deep breaths and allow yourself to relax.

As you breathe deeply, try to let go of all the emotions you are holding onto. With each breath, you try to let yourself go more and more, and as you let go, you realize that everything around you is made of love. Allow yourself to live within this love.

If you practice these techniques of positive thinking, you will be able to connect with the flow of life and you will find more luck than you have ever had.

CHAPTER 15: The way of Success

The only strategy for success is to define it priori.. Otherwise, your life will remain a constant do-do-do without goals. I realize it's not easy, but with a little practice you will be able to understand what is really important to you and how to get there. I've been working on it for a long time and I haven't finished my drawing yet. It is not easy; it requires application and flexibility because the objectives can change over the years and indeed do change. Making explicit what's important is relatively simple, but understanding what your priorities are and how to organize yourself to achieve your goals requires dedication. Above all, it implies learning to say *no*.

The preparation

Before even defining your goals, you must put yourself in a position to recognize them. Withdraw from the world enough for you to focus on your ego, to use an Indian metaphor. You need to be able to perceive your existence at the level of consciousness and being. Only by separating the two factors, will you be able to determine your path. You need to be able to rationalize what you are doing in your life, starting to line up the dots. How did you get to your current position? Where did you start from? How many times and why have you taken turns and how many times have you limited yourself to seizing opportunities? Did you choose to be who you are or did you become this by chance?

Nurture your own passions, not sell them for a job

In my life I have changed activities three times: I went from working as a freelance journalist to writing for a newspaper. I went back to freelancing and now I also work as a communications consultant. I have not always chosen myself, even if the direction I managed to keep has always been in line with my goals.

I like to write and I love football: He will be a sports journalist; I told myself, when it came to choosing the university. I was wrong and not a little. In order to try to "work" in a sector that I liked, I then found myself sacrificing my passions at work. What I have learned is that one's passions must be fed independently.

This is how after having worked as a freelance journalist first and as an employee, I finally started writing on my own. The worst that happened to me? Following football matches for work, because this has taken away from my experience as a sportsman, the pleasure of following the match.

In retrospect, I can tell you that if I started entrusting my thoughts on the subject to a personal blog today, I would probably be paid to continue doing so. It is not presumption, since they then paid me for something not too different.

If I had cultivated my passion without offering it in exchange for a salary, I would have been paid not to do a job, but to continue to follow my passion.

Meditate on an action plan

All this is clear to you only when you define your success priori. I like to take a formula proposed by David Allen in Getting Things Done and apply it even more for that purpose. I tell you what I'm doing now and what I think you should do too. You split your consciousness. Now, imagine parachuting into your life from the top of an airplane while slowly descending.

At 50,000 you see yourself in the world: What role do you occupy? Instead, where would you have wanted to be? How do you want to be perceived by others? What do you want them to say at your funeral? What do you want people to remember you for?

At 40,000 feet, you must understand the operations to be performed to move your ego from where it is and get it to where you would like to see it at the final whistle.

At 30,000 feet, you see everything closer and you are able to start planning, identifying the steps to take to reach the goal. It will be easier for you to do this if you have tried to connect the dots before, making it clear how you found yourself where you are now.

At 20,000 feet, you start to lose the overview, but if you've made it clear before, you can now focus on the piece of road you are taking, planning the route to take to get to the next point, which can be five to ten years away.

At 10,000 feet, it's about better defining the stretch you need to grind over the next few years, the one you have in front of you.

Once you land, all you have to do is focus on the steps you are taking, since those to be taken should be clear to you by now.

Two ways to achieve the vision of together

In my experience, there are at least two ways that work to define the way forward. They are meditation and the journaling.

Meditation

By meditation, I don't mean an ascetic practice to reach the supreme state, but the act of continually thinking exclusively about what you want to achieve. By identifying above all the things to say no to get to the goal. Just as in traditional meditation, the focus on your breath brings you back to concentration, so in your life you must find the fixed point to return to when other thoughts distract you. Your core business, if you want. An exercise easy and yet very useful is to start with the list of useless things you do every day. Every time you turn on the TV to see what's on, for example, you're just wasting your time, because you didn't decide to watch some show for your own interest, but your only decision was to switch off your brain.

-

You can meditate in different ways. Two tools that I find very functional are:

Relaxing deeply helps you focus on yourself, one problem at a time. When you are focused, you can start thinking about the path you are taking. The trick is to hold onto the breath as a tool to return to our thinking when the mind tries to wander. Starting from a form of meditation helps you in two respects: Firstly, it allows you to find time to think, relaxing, and secondly it allows you to identify a specific space-time for your reflections.

Running, walking or otherwise exercising, preferably outdoors also help. Most of the sports activities is based on the concept of habit, articulated trigger, work done on automatic pilot and awards. When you run, your brain orders your body to perform a certain type of operation in sequence, without you having to worry about conscious thinking. At that moment, the creative side takes over. Decide the problem that must be solved or question you want to answer and put a run. I have tried it several times. This has now become an essential tool for planning my activities.

The journaling

In Italian, we would say "keeping a diary", but translating the term, I seem to lose the deeper aspect of this operation. By forcing yourself to shape your thoughts, you will find yourself having more to do with them, analyzing them deeply and exposing them. Writing stimulates the creative part of your brain in an unconscious way. Rereading what you have written helps you to better understand your approach to a given theme, so as to rework it and deepen it.

A practical guide

I would like to suggest this to you, to begin with. It starts on Monday. It takes a week.

As soon as you wake up, go out for a walk or run of at least half an hour. The goal of this activity is to define the six levels of in-depth study I wrote to you earlier. Observe your life from 50,000 feet up to the ground.

During the day, find ten minutes to meditate. This is a physical exercise that will help you focus on yourself. Don't forget this part. If you take it as a habit, it will become extremely useful. You can plan your activities so that you do it the night before the journaling.

In the evening, take half an hour to write down what you thought while running and meditating. Write without worrying about the form and what you write. Write freely, you are doing it for yourself and no one else.

Rest on the seventh day. You will realize that you have missed these activities and will gladly return to them. Sunday is the day dedicated to rereading what you have written. Again, don't worry about the shape or anything else. Read to inquire about your thoughts. Take notes, if you can think of something to do. They will be a great starting point for your next runs, meditations and scriptures.

Conclusion

LIFE AS A SINGLE

The psychologist Donald Winnicott said that being alone is a sign of great maturity.

A child is completely dependent on his parents, but as he grows up, he becomes more and more independent.

Growing up, the individual learns to make sense of his life and comes to no longer have to depend on others to define it.

Who said that singles are necessarily sad, lonely and obsessed with the search for their soul mate?

A study carried out at the University of California breaks down these stereotypes and argues that lonely hearts have the power to make independent choices and are more prone to face and overcome life's problems than those who are married.

It emerged that singles are more likely to experience continuous inner growth and less likely to experience negative emotions, than colleagues who live in a loving relationship.

It seems that singles also tend to give greater value to work and are able to dedicate themselves more consistently and diligently to family, friends, neighbors and acquaintances.

Those who have always thought that marriage makes people happier and more willing to surround themselves with other individuals will have to change their mind. Through the study conducted, it is argued that married people are more prone to isolation than singles.

Singles seem to live a fuller, more authentic and meaningful life precisely because they live alone. A single person can do anything without accountability to anyone. They sleep better. It is scientifically proven that single people rest better if they sleep alone.

This means you have more room to move around, you don't hear anyone snoring, you stay in bed longer and have more energy in the morning.

You can leave when and where you want.

Not giving an account to anyone also means putting two swimsuits in your backpack and going to visit your friend in a nearby capital for the weekend, without someone going crazy with jealousy.

Being in order and looking good is a commitment that you make with yourself and not for someone else.

You can focus on your career. Having an important story is challenging. It must be admitted. When you meet the person of your life, you are certainly ready to make every sacrifice to make the story last and oftentimes, it doesn't even weigh. But, as long as you are single and you don't meet the person who makes us feel "light", even when you are about to take out a mortgage for a semi-detached house, it is better to focus on professional success.

You have more time for friends. Engaged friends will say that it is not true, that they are always there for you. Too bad that when you call to improvise an aperitif, they always have a commitment already made, which they cannot move.

You raise your self-esteem by getting by on your own. You learn to distinguish the moments when you can ask someone for help and those when you have to rely only on yourself. You know yourself better and deeper, because you face your fears alone.

One is the creator of one's own happiness. Your mood does not depend on someone else. You learn about your sadness, your ups and downs, and to react positively.

One can be "selfish" without guilt. You can make your own plans, change them and reciprocate them without having to justify them to someone and without having to adapt them to the wishes of another.

You can go out whenever you want, with whoever you want.

You can eat when hungry.

In single life, people tend to exercise more. A study of 13,000 Americans, ages 18 to 64, revealed that those who have never been married, engage in more physical activity than those in the other categories (divorced / separated, married, widower), regardless of age and gender. Exercise is directly linked to other health benefits, such as improved mood, increased energy levels, better sleep quality, improved cardiovascular activity, and even better sexual performance.

You are more socially active. Some experts say that singles are more resilient and that they are able to forge stronger social bonds than married people because they seek more opportunities to socialize.

We tend to eat healthier. There are several scientific studies that attest to the benefits of a peaceful relationship, but living an unhealthy, toxic or divorced relationship is harmful to both the mind and the body. Ill and unhappy relationships can lead to a variety of behaviors and harmful habits, such as "comfort feasting" (eating everything and gaining weight, because you are looking for a "friend", for comfort) and "control feasting" (using food deprivation to control something in your life), as sex and relationship expert Laurel House explains.

Friendships last longer. Even if you don't want to, many friendships take a back seat when you get married. Priorities become mate and family. That's right, but on the other hand, singles tend to keep their friendships standing and this makes them "better" friends. If you can count on a group of important people, your life will not fall apart when the "right one" is gone.

Less debts accumulate. Money isn't worth as much health and happiness, but debt is stressful. It seems that singles tend to have less. While money issues cause a lot of stress and stress can damage health, this is indeed an important discovery.

You become self-sufficient. Alone, you learn to enjoy time only for yourself. The ability to live independently, with fulfillment is an important "survival technique" that not all people in a couple are able to enjoy.

You must not give up on anything and you are not afraid of causing quarrels, misunderstandings and separations.

The single person doesn't need to lie to anyone, they live their life exactly as it is.

In a relationship, compromises are fundamental. Alone, they aren't.

Being alone is necessary

Spending time alone is essential to regain balance, especially in those moments when you feel overloaded. Several tests confirm that being alone causes important changes in the brain, in terms of thoughts and emotions.

Even if being alone has always been a fundamental need, in our century, we are witnessing an increase in the value attributed to social relations. Although being alone with ourselves brings well-being, the general perception is often that of a situation to be feared and a source of distress. Various meditation practices require spending time alone.

Some of them plan to stay a few days in total solitude and absolute silence, avoiding any contact with the outside world. Would you be able to handle this? Most people may not be willing to handle such a situation. This is because we are not used to receiving such a low level of stimulation. Isolating yourself and not experiencing any contact for any length of time is a real test of fire.

To be able to be alone, you need training. Yet, if this test is so common among those who meditate, it is precisely because it brings great benefits. Loneliness, if well managed, makes you stronger.

Company overwhelms sometimes.

Social relationships demand a lot from us, especially when they are many and important. At the same time, however, they generate great satisfaction. Yet, without even realizing it, they can turn into situations that can take away time and energy.

Very easily, we end up living according to others. Work, partner, family, friends—there are many social areas in which we move daily, all with specific needs and tensions. Many times, we come to a point where we are unable to distinguish where our personal sphere ends and where that of others begins, or vice versa. Being alone is a way to focus our attention and energy on ourselves; an opportunity to be "selfish" without feeling guilty. These spaces help us to find ourselves again—perceive how we really are, when we are not immersed in our usual context.

Time alone raises awareness

Somehow, even loneliness requires silence. In fact, there is a shift of attention from outside to inside. By ceasing to use the part of the brain that is in charge of speech, other areas begin to increase their intensity. There is evidence of how attention and concentration become more powerful. In solitude, thought is sharpened and ingenuity is refined. Thoughts may seem confusing at first, but they will soon begin to take on a well-defined form. Being alone for several days generates a sensitizing effect; that is, we begin to realize ideas and feelings that we were not aware of before. It is a way of awakening by increasing our connection with ourselves.

-

Being alone and the effects on the brain

Some studies show that loneliness and silence are good for the folds of the cerebral cortex. Apparently, this benefit increases the thickness of the gray matter. The result is that we become more adept at processing information.

All of this have a more than positive impact on our cognitive processes. When we return to our normal life, we notice that we are able to learn and memorize more easily. This is good for any intellectual activity, making us more productive. At the same time, it is very likely that in those moments of loneliness, the so-called "Eureka moments" appear. Let's talk about instant inspirations. In other words, all the conditions that facilitate the stimulation of creativity.

Singles Are Not Sad, A Research Flips A Secular Stereotype

Singles say everything. They are now being pointed out almost as much as vegans and homosexuals. Those who choose to live a single life (and not have children) are said to be "a very selfish person." An egoism that hides, always according to common sense, a great sadness.

Before we begin, I emphasize that this chapter is not intended to exalt the lonely lifestyle and belittle that of a couple. The sole purpose of this paragraph is to illustrate the results of recent research which suggests that, the myths of singles being sad is wrong. On the contrary, they are very happy. Research dismantles all stereotypes about singles. Singles are still "victims" of die-hard stereotypes. To remedy this, researchers at the University of California have decided to carry out a research to dismantle each stereotype piece by piece.

1. It is not true that they are sad and lonely

The myth of sad and lonely singles, desperate for a palliative to remedy the absence of a soul mate, is hard to die; it turns out that single people are more open to experiences than those who have chosen life as a couple, and have a greater sense of self-determination.

A study shows that psychic self-sufficiency is a great advantage of singles. What does this term mean? Psychic self-sufficiency is feeling confident and satisfied with oneself. It is a profound sense of completeness and inner stability.

Jamila Bookwala, professor at LaFayette College (Easton, USA), compared 1,486 married people with 105 never married people, all over 40 years of age. His goal was to understand, among other things, what difference there was in this aspect of well-being. Comparisons showed that the more self-sufficient people were, the less likely they were to experience negative emotions. Singles proved to be more self-reliant, therefore, less likely to experience negative emotions. The curious thing is that for married people, the opposite was true. According to DePaulo: The more a married person proved self-sufficient, the more he suffered from it.

2. Satisfied with living alone

By now, the derogatory use of words such as "bachelor" or "spinster" is about to set. When interviewed, singles say they are satisfied not to share the house and daily life with someone. At the same time, they say that they would not change this idea if they found a mate or a partner. At least, that's what they say. Maybe, once they get engaged, they may change their mind and feel more satisfied with someone around.

3. Singles care about personal growth

Those who live alone demonstrate a propensity for personal growth and psychological development. By personal growth, we mean "that particular form of human development that allows people to discover their potential, often present, but unexpressed." Learning to communicate effectively, gaining problem-solving skills by adopting new perspectives and learning to assert yourself by becoming persuasive, are all examples of personal growth. Those who achieve these and other achievements are more likely to become successful, rich and famous. Singles seem to be more inclined to personal growth and are more oriented towards greater psychological development. They love to invest their time and savings on themselves, not to gain momentary, futile satisfaction, but to become better individuals—like any person with common sense, regardless of marital status.

4. Their friendships last longer

Even if they don't want to, when people get married, they lose many friendships, as they put them in the background. Priorities become partner and family. In an article titled "Marriage: The good, the ugly and the greedy", published in the scientific Sage Journal, sociologists Naomi Gerstel and Natalia Sarkisian illustrate the unwanted effects of marriage and how the latter can break the social ties of the spouses. On the other hand, singles are more capable of keeping their friendships standing and this makes them "best" friends.

5. Are you single by choice or because society has abandoned us?

Is single life a choice or a necessity? There is still no clear figure. While it is true that many young people declare that they undertake a solitary life to cultivate their personal growth, it is also true that the elderly regret the choice of not having surrounded themselves with significant people. The Censis researchers, who periodically analyze these phenomena say, it is no longer just the effect of the general aging of the population, or the consequent loss of relationships due to death, but there are new social phenomena taking place. In summary, the research sends a message: There is no better life plan than another.

Printed in Great Britain
by Amazon

61201410R00111